You don't just need a logo, you need a legacy.

WIN YOUR BRAND!

The Unapologetic Playbook for Becoming Iconic

I0536156

Samara Beth
(a.k.a. "Badass Bamboo")

Integrity Publishing International LLC

Copyright © 2025

Published by Integrity Publishing International LLC
www.IntegrityPub.com

WIN YOUR BRAND | SAMARA BETH

Orders by U.S. trade bookstores and wholesalers.

Email: *Team@IntegrityPub.com*

Paperback ISBN: 978-1-964330-36-5
Hardback ISBN: 978-1-964330-37-2

Includes Brand Bonus - Samara Beth shares her WINNING Brand Framework secrets of going from invisible to iconic, and everything in between.

WIN

The
Unapologetic
Playbook
for
Becoming
Iconic

YOUR
BRAND

SAMARA BETH

Foreword by Jim Cathcart

Testimonials

"Samara Beth's WIN Your Brand is a masterclass in unapologetic authenticity, showing how purpose-driven connection is the true currency of influence. Her W.I.N. Framework transforms branding from a marketing tactic into a movement of impact, service, and legacy. This book is a must-read for anyone who wants to elevate their brand by elevating others first."

— **David Meltzer,** Co-Founder of Sports 1 Marketing, Speaker, Author & Podcast Host

"Samara Beth always brings massive energy and freshness to every project. She finds ways to help each person in her path discover how to get the most from the world. She will definitely open your eyes to new ways of finding your next journey!"

— **Kane & Alessia Minkus,** Partners, **Industry Rockstar,** Award-Winning Serial Entrepreneurs, International Bestselling Authors, & World-Renowned Business Mentors with Expertise in AI

"I met Samara Beth several years ago at a 10X event, and from the second she walked into the room, she lit it up. She's one of the kindest, most genuine people I've ever met—and I know Win Your Brand will be just like her: real, powerful, and unforgettable. I truly can't wait to read it."

— **Tom Carter,** CEO, 4Winners Merch

"Samara Beth's WIN Your Brand is pure gold for entrepreneurs who want to amplify their influence and create deeper emotional connections with their audiences. Her W.I.N. Framework is the perfect blend of strategy, storytelling, and heart. Samara doesn't just talk about building a brand; I have seen her live it with authenticity and fire. This book is your roadmap to standing out, serving boldly, and winning big."

— **Todd Hartley,** Founder of The WireBuzz Revenue Acceleration Agency and a Tony Robbins Business Mastery Faculty Speaker

"Samara Beth's WIN Your Brand is a breath of fresh air in a world full of filters and facades. She reminds us that authenticity isn't just attractive—it's magnetic. As someone who's built a career in television and storytelling, I couldn't agree more: being real and true to yourself and your audience is what makes you truly likable and unforgettable, whether it's on camera, in a book, or behind the mic. Samara's playbook shows exactly how to do that with grace, grit, and undeniable charisma."

— **Barbara Majeski,** American Television Personality, Philanthropist, & Lifestyle Expert

"Partnering with Samara Beth & Co. has empowered me to elevate my standards, refine my professionalism, and deepen my confidence. Samara's guidance in such a short time has been invaluable, and I'm excited for everything we will continue to build."

— **Araceli Salazar,** Fashion Designer, founder of the ARACELI Designs

"Samara Beth is the Quintessential Queen of Branding. If you desire getting noticed in a noisy viral world without being drowned out in whispers of 'I don't know them, why should I work with them?' Hire Samara Beth to take your personal brand, business, or team brand to the next dimension. She puts you into all the places and spaces you need to be in to win."

— **Arthur Superman Barnes,** The Brain Evangelist, Unbeatable Entrepreneur & Destiny Disruptor

"I've had the pleasure of getting to know Samara Beth through events and programs, and what stands out most about her is her genuine energy and passion for helping others rise. WIN Your Brand is a powerful reflection of who she is—bold, intentional, and deeply committed to empowering others to own their story. I truly believe in this book and the transformation it will bring to anyone ready to step into their next level with confidence and purpose."

— **Lindsey Marie,** Founder of Powerhouse Women & host of the Powerhouse Women Podcast

"WIN Your Brand is a refreshing, no-fluff roadmap for building a purpose-driven business that aligns heart and strategy. Samara Beth brings soul to branding, teaching you how to lead with integrity, connection, and confidence while turning your story into lasting impact. Her W.I.N. Framework is exactly what today's entrepreneurs need to rise above noise and build something truly iconic."

— **Kelly Resendez,** President of Menrva, Strategic Advisor GoodLeap, Co-Founder Gobundance Women, Author and Podcast Host Power Up Your Life

9

"WIN Your Brand is a book not only timely in its message, but essential in today's business landscape. The bar for the absolute minimum requirements keeps changing—and that direction is never down. It isn't just about what you do anymore, as much as it is about who you are. We must not lose sight of the importance of what is unique about you. That's your personal brand. Craft it wisely and with intention, and it can both guide you and inspire others in the midst of the growing chaos and uncertainty of modern times."

— **Dr. David Owers,** Doctor, MedCenter Owner, Author, Coach

"Samara Beth teaches you how to win in your brand as well as how to win in your life! As a Speaker and Habits Coach who has spent decades on stages around the world, I can assure you her W.I.N. framework is the real deal. It's unapologetic, authentic, and completely aligned with serving others first. If you're ready to step into your iconic self without drama and with massive impact, this book is your next dose of AWESOME!"

— **Erik "Mr. Awesome" Swanson,** Award-Winning International Keynote Speaker & Multi-Time #1 International Bestselling Author

"I've had the rare privilege of working with Samara Beth; nothing about her is ordinary. Her presence is electric, her creativity is boundless, and her resilience is quietly fierce. She doesn't just elevate brands; she elevates people with truth, purpose, and a deep understanding of what it means to lead authentically. "W.I.N. your Brand" captures the essence of who Samara Beth is: a force of transformation whose life

10

experience becomes fuel for yours. If you are ready to meet the most powerful version of yourself, start with this book, and let Samara Beth show you the way. This is where your real story begins."

— **Viktoria Danchuk Verstria,** Synergy Systems Architect

"What I know to be true and factual is that Samara is an example and testament to what strength, endurance, and grit are, and is equally as kind, caring, and believes in being of service to those who are blessed to cross her path. She is human and, when required, a superhuman. She has lived and experienced, and still lives with integrity and love. This is why I would give and do anything for Samara because she would do it for me. I am grateful to have her in my life."

— **Jason Jimenez,** CEO, Landing Big Whales

"I first met Samara Beth on the Clubhouse social audio app in 2020, when the world was in chaos, and connection meant everything. Through our collaboration in Landing Big Whales and our shared journey in the 10X community, I witnessed firsthand the strength, passion, and authenticity that define who she is—both on and off the stage.

Samara Beth has faced a lifetime of adversity and somehow turned every challenge into fuel for growth. She doesn't just bounce back; she rises higher every single time. Her story is one of grit, grace, and heart—a rare combination that makes her not only an extraordinary coach and leader, but an even more remarkable human being. In Win Your Brand, Samara gives readers the exact tools and mindset that helped her rebuild, reinvent, and rise. It's more than a branding guide—

it's a roadmap for resilience, purpose, and unapologetic authenticity. She embodies what it means to live 10X in every area of life, and this book captures that spirit perfectly."

— **Cherrie Sacchetti,** President & CEO, Victress Group

"Samara Beth brings the same kind of grit and resilience it took me to fight my way into the UFC in less than a year. WIN Your Brand isn't just a book—it's a battle plan for leaders and creators to rise."

— **Clifford Starks,** UFC Fighter, Business Coach

"Samara Beth has been a valued part of the Owwll community for years, always showing up for me and our members countless times. She has helped grow our community in meaningful ways while also assisting others in need, sparking connections that truly change lives. Her energy, authenticity, and resilience inspire action, and her W.I.N. framework is more than a strategy—it's a life philosophy that empowers entrepreneurs and leaders to rise above challenges and build brands with purpose. This book is a must-read for anyone ready to reach their full potential."

— **Jason Hill,** Founder of *Owwll* app

"I've known Samara for thirty-nine years. Samara's style, energy, and beauty amazed me then and still do to this day. However, it is her heart, her optimism, and her spirit that are why we love her so very much."

— **Jason Ott,** Attorney-at-Law

"Samara is such a kind, generous, thoughtful, and welcoming person! She is full of great energy and chooses to surround herself with people who lift her up to be better. I'm privileged to know her as a person, and I know having her in my life makes me a better person, friend, wife, and mother."

— **Holly Close,** Fellow Navy Submarine Spouse, Former Ombudsman

"Samara Beth and I worked together producing events for clients and associations. I always found her to have creative ideas, a positive attitude, and to be an enthusiastic advocate for her cause. Her ability to organize and prioritize what needed to be done was spot on! She partnered with her vendors and colleagues to present logical, financially sound, and fun solutions. Personally, I would enjoy opportunities to work with her."

— **Margery Reinheardt, CPCE,** Retired from Hilton Hotels

"I met Samara during the pandemic on an audio app that went viral during the lockdown in 2020. We spent quite a bit of time in business-related rooms and realized that we had more in common than different. I created my speaking platform shortly after and invited her to speak, which she did amazingly on several occasions. I also supported her event planning training. I would highly recommend that you read the W.I.N. Your Brand book because she is definitely going to over-deliver on the value, knowledge, and her expertise."

— **Ramona Rogers,** Serial Entrepreneur, Speaker, Coach, Author

"Samara Beth is a force of energy, resilience, and raw authenticity. I've witnessed her unwavering commitment to helping others rise, and WIN Your Brand is a testament to that purpose. This book is not just a guide, it's a spark for anyone ready to show up boldly, lead with purpose, and build a brand that thrives through any storm. Proud to call her a friend and a powerhouse in motion."

— **Jaikishaan Sharma,** Mindset Coach & Speaker

"I am proud to endorse, Samara Beth and her remarkable new book. She is the true definition of resilience—a go-getter and a reinvention maverick who continually transforms challenges into opportunities for growth and success. Her story and insights are a testament to her courage, creativity, and relentless drive to inspire others.

This book is more than a reflection of her journey—it's a roadmap for anyone seeking to reinvent themselves with purpose and passion. Samara has lived what she writes, and that authenticity shines through on every page."

— **Judy Oppel,** Director of Projects, American Friends of the Uffizi Galleries

"Samara Beth has a way of bringing her whole self to any circumstance. Her energy is infectious, and you'll feel like you've known her forever in short order."

— **Amy Fiore,** Theatre Director

"Samara Beth is an absolute gem—brilliant, resilient, and full of heart. Like all precious gems, she's been forged under pressure, and each challenge has only made her shine brighter. Her journey is one of grit, grace, and unshakable warmth, and this book reflects the same spirit: real, radiant, and impossible to forget. To know Samara is to know true friendship, feel like family, fierce determination, and the kind of love that lifts others higher."

— **Chelsea Lumaque,** BSN-RN

"I have watched Samara rise through moments that would have stopped most people, and she kept finding a way to move forward. She leads with heart, grit, and a kind of resilience that comes from real lived experience. She is such a beautiful human, and her story will encourage anyone who needs to remember their own strength."

— **Rob Actis,** Author of "The Law of Action," known to many as "The Podcast Whisperer"

"I've known Samara Beth for over a decade, and from the very beginning, I was touched by her enthusiasm and her passion. She's a freaking force of nature. She's taken every punch that life threw at her and turned the bruises into fuel. Trust me, she's gonna do it all with a smile.

I'm very proud of you, my friend. You are a real warrior and an inspiration for many of us."

— **Carolina Polanco,** Friend

"I have witnessed Samara Beth at her lowest mentally, emotionally, and physically. Through the process of embodying her trapped emotions, sitting in the pain, I have joyfully seen her blossom into a vibrant, healed, powerful woman through her willingness to feel, accept, forgive, and let go. I recommend following Samara's journey and learn from her resilience and action."

— **Dr. Bryan Geier,** a.k.a. "Dr. Fascia"

"Samara Beth is a tornado of passion formed into focused and impactful leadership! In 'WIN YOUR BRAND,' she shows by example how to elevate your message—and your life!

Samara is a resilient and relentless example of the grit we need more of, not only to inspire but also to bring us together and transcend the darkened divisiveness that has no place in real leadership. As someone who has spent a lifetime helping others rise, Samara has learned through the predictable mistakes we make up the awkward path up Destiny's Mountain of compassion and impact. I salute a humble, devoted heart that will help you carve a brand that has real impact, and one that stands tall through the storms of life. So please read this book!

Expanding how we see ourselves, and see the enormous capacity in all we meet, we change by definition WHAT IS POSSIBLE!"

— **Nick Lowery,** NFL KC Chiefs Hall of Fame, Founder of Champions for The Homeless, Harvard MPA and Human Potential Advocate, Author of "Naked and Alone with 80,000 People"

"I've known Samara Beth since we were eleven years old, and her strength, heart, and determination have always been undeniable. WIN YOUR BRAND captures the resilience and brilliance she's carried through every chapter of her life, turning challenges into purpose and purpose into impact. This book is Samara—authentic, courageous, and unstoppable—and it will inspire anyone who reads it to rise higher."

— **Stephanie Silberstein,** Theatre Director, Actor, Teacher, Writer, Coach, Standup Comedian

DEDICATION

This book is dedicated to the loves of my life.

To my daddy, whose memory fuels my drive and reminds me that true legacy is built in moments, not money.

To my mom, whose strength, laughter, and endless love keep me anchored through life's wild roller coasters.

To my son, whose courage and passions inspire me daily as he faces every obstacle with an unwavering heart.

To my daughter, whose spark of ambition, creativity, and friendship fills my world with pride and light.

To my big brothers who are there for me whenever I call.

And to my best friend, through thick and thin, whose steady presence and quiet wisdom make every challenge softer to bear. I'm endlessly grateful for the love poured into creating my book cover.

I am blessed to have love surrounding me in my life—past, present, and always.

Contents

A NOTE ABOUT THE AUTHOR

As someone who's walked beside, overseen, and helped Samara build her company from scratch, with multiple pivots (the ones no one sees behind the scenes), I have witnessed firsthand what *true resilience* looks like. When most would have stopped, she found another gear. When the world went quiet, she kept moving.

She's the kind of person I love to work with: brave, relentless, grounded, and fiercely heart-led. She moves through the world with a rare blend of empathy and edge, where compassion fuels discipline.

"WIN YOUR BRAND" isn't just a book, it's her philosophy in motion. A manual for anyone who's ever felt like giving up, yet chose to rise again. This isn't just about winning in business, it's about showing up and winning in life, even when all the odds seem to be stacked against you.

Although I call Samara "Badass Bamboo," she'll always be "Little Bamboo" to me: the one who bends, but never breaks. Her strength lies in her softness, her power in her persistence.

This book captures that essence—it's equal parts heart, hustle, and healing.

Samara reminds us that the business you build starts long before the logo, it begins in the fire you refuse to walk away from, in the moments you refuse to give up and in the relentless decision to keep showing up.

Justine Pogroske
Founder & CEO, Million Dollar Branders

WELCOME TO MY BAMBOO FOREST: WHERE YOU WIN YOUR BRAND

I whispered the same sentence to myself over and over:

"I can't do this again."

"I can't do this again."

"I can't do this again."

I was standing in my new home office of my thirtieth home with stacks of boxes, repeating the words of negative thoughts and energy, like I was in shock. I had just moved in that morning. It was just hours after my dad had a stroke.

Eight weeks later, we lost him, and I restarted anyway. If you've ever had to rebuild your life, business, or identity, you know the truth: Reinvention feels impossible—right up until the moment you choose it. I don't identify with steel or stone. I identify with bamboo—nature's paradox of strength. It bends; it doesn't break. Especially in storms.

The storms come in cycles: Economies, wars, tariffs, divorces, floods—sometimes all at once. I've lived through more than a few. Yet there's a rhythm to resilience. You ride the ebbs and flows, and you keep creating. Even now, in the year 2025, when this book is written, as artificial intelligence reshapes our world in real time, the work is to adapt without abandoning who you are. I quadrupled my production in a few months using a handful of tools. The irony? That only puts you back at average. Everyone else is running, too.

This book is an unapologetic guide to becoming iconic. Not insta-famous, not glossy, but iconic. It's built from decades of producing experiences for global brands, winning stages, and navigating life's messiest plot twists. It's built on WIN: Willpower to keep going when it feels impossible, Innovation to think creatively and act decisively, and Networking to build a community that can actually hold you when the winds pick up. Bamboo isn't delicate. It's designed to sway and survive. So are you.

What if I told you that some of your hardest moments—the heartbreaks, the sudden moves, the sleepless nights, the quiet sacrifices—weren't setbacks, but soil? What if the chaos, the grief, and the uncertainty were the very conditions your growth required?

That's what I learned.

Not all at once. Not gracefully—and not without scars. It's not to say I am out of the forest for good, either.

But through it all—from motherhood and military life to raising a son with autism, a miscarriage, losing a child, reinvention, entrepreneurship, and being forced to start over more times than I can count, I found something unshakable: *my roots*. And even more powerfully: *my flexibility*. The kind of strength that doesn't look like steel. It looks like bamboo.

Bamboo is one of the fastest-growing plants in the world, but it doesn't shoot up overnight. For years, it grows roots underground, unseen, before ever sprouting above the surface. That image stuck with me because I realized I'd spent so much of my life building invisible roots, weathering storms others never saw, preparing for the moment I would grow tall and strong. Funny, how I used the word "stuck" multiple times when talking about Coach Ron Tunick. He used to say, "If you are stuck in life or business, you have no dream."

Scholar and author Karen Salmansohn wrote, "Bamboo bends in the wind, but never breaks, because it is flexible." That became my rallying cry. Flexibility isn't weakness. It's resilience. And resilience, paired with grit and grace, is what I teach through "The Badass Bamboo Theory." This methodology shows that bending in life's storms allows us not just to survive, but to thrive and build a legacy that lasts long after we're gone.

That's where this journey begins—with a metaphor and a mission.

You're holding a book that is part memoir, part manifesto, and part blueprint. It's a love letter to every person who's ever felt overlooked, underestimated, or uprooted. It's a wake-up call to the coach who's quietly rebuilding, the corporate employee ready to pivot, the entrepreneur who knows he or she is meant for more, the resilient industry business owner who is tired of the world's politics, weather, and economy negatively impacting their business.

And it's also a tool.

Because *Samara Beth* isn't just about where I've been (13 cities, 30 homes, thousands of stories). It's about where you're going, how you are winning with your personal or business brand, and how to keep reaching out everywhere you need to be.

WHY THIS BOOK? WHY NOW?

After spending decades producing award-winning social and corporate events, consulting for Fortune 500 brands, building and closing businesses across borders, and setting the stages for powerhouse names, I realized that my story wasn't just mine. It was a mirror. A reminder that reinvention isn't reserved for the lucky or the privileged. It's a *process*. And I had lived it on repeat.

This book is designed to give you both the inspiration and the strategy to turn your resilience into *revenue*, your recovery into *reinvention*, and your setbacks into *stages*.

INTRODUCING THE BADASS BAMBOO THEORY

The Badass Bamboo Theory is my personal philosophy—and now, my professional methodology—for how to rise, lead, and thrive no matter the weather. It's built around my W.I.N. Framework:

- **Willpower** – Harnessing grit and grace to move forward even when the path disappears.

- **Innovation** – Creatively adapting, evolving, and boldly pivoting without apology.

- **Networking** – Building circles that elevate you, challenge you, and keep you rooted.

You'll see how I applied this in my own life. From struggles with education and sacrifices as a Navy wife to burying a child, building a nationally recognized brand while mothering two incredible kids (aged fifteen and twenty-one when this book was written), reinventing my identity in every new zip code, and overcoming the challenges of divorce after a twenty-two-year marriage.

THIS IS ABOUT YOU, TOO

Yes, this is my story. But it's written for you.

You, the person standing at a crossroads.

You, the entrepreneur craving clarity.

You, the working mom or single parent, who keeps showing up even when no one sees the invisible load.

You don't need to be perfect. You don't need more time. You just need to start where you are, and root deeply into who you're becoming.

If I can rise from the bottom of the barrel with a bank account near empty, credit cards maxed, credit score tanked, dreams on pause, self-worth shaken, and create a business, brand, and legacy that touches lives, you can, too.

This is your invitation to rise, sway, root, stretch, and multiply. Resilience isn't hardening. It's engineered flexibility.

LET'S *WIN* YOUR BRAND, TOGETHER

This book is also the foundation for the movement behind *Samara Beth & Co.*, a global platform where I coach entrepreneurs, executives, authors, coaches, and companies to elevate their brands, command stages, produce impactful events, and create unforgettable client experiences.

Whether you're a speaker, service provider, sales representative, or corporate executive officer, I'll show you how to build a brand that bends without breaking and grows without limits.

Because you don't need another blueprint written by someone who's never weathered a storm.

You need a guide who *is* the storm… and the stunning sunset that comes after.

Let's begin.

With love & grit,

— **Samara Beth**

a.k.a. "Badass Bamboo"

JIM CATHCART

THE WILL TO WIN

"Just remember in the winter, far beneath the bitter snow,
lies a seed that,
with the sun's love, in the Spring becomes the Rose."
The Rose, as sung by Bette Midler

There is a seed deep inside you that is your true nature. It holds the potential of millions of trees and forests that will echo throughout time. Just like an acorn, you carry a legacy from the past generations, plus protective guidance from your mentors, teachers, parents, role models, and guides.

You also carry the potential to imprint the world for generations. You were intentionally created—not just by your parents but by your Creator. You are meant to exist, and you have a contribution to give.

Never think of yourself as small or insignificant. Remember that seed, know that you have a job to do, a contribution to give. We, the rest of the world, need what you are here to give. Don't deny us your contribution by thinking small and living without meaning. Nurture your dreams, keep the flame alive, know that your day is coming, again and again. If you are still breathing, then your work is not complete.

Samara Beth speaks of the metaphor of Bamboo; how it seemingly sleeps in the ground for long periods of time only to emerge in a powerful burst of steady growth and lasting resilience. That is you. You aren't done yet.

The Structure of this book is WIN: Willpower, Innovation and Networking.

Willpower is misunderstood. People think willpower is simply steely resolve to keep going no matter what. I disagree. They say you must have The Will To Win! I somewhat disagree.

Perseverance does not come from desire nor power from within you. It is a symptom of your commitment to make your dream a reality. It is your willingness to keep showing up even when you don't see progress… yet.

The reason you would commit to keep going toward a dream is because you have faith that it could happen. Faith is trusting in things that are not yet proven. Read that again.

Do you believe in God? In Thought? In Love? None of these are known through tangible reality, though reality certainly makes the case for them. Each of them requires us to suspend our demand for hard evidence and believe in the concept behind them. God isn't seen in traditional ways, yet there are miracles throughout creation to affirm His existence. Thought is assumed to exist but we can't see or touch it. Love is known by all who have experienced it, but none have ever seen it.

Your dreams are like that. They don't yet exist in tangible reality, but they have the power to pull you forward. They make you persist against resistance. But dreams must be clear and generate feelings in order to become magnets for our achievement.

The Will to Win is meaningless without the Will to Train and Prepare. Everyone has a "desire" to win, but will is stronger than desire. We need the Will to Learn, to Grow, to Endure, to Sustain, to Train and Prepare. Then we will Win, not before.

Innovation comes from the root word "Nova" or new. It's been said that there is nothing new under the sun. Maybe that's true for the basic elements of science, but new combinations and applications occur every day.

Disneyland was a combination of state fairs, carnivals, botanical gardens, movie theaters, Broadway theaters, and birthday parties. It was none of these, but it was also all of them. It was new.

Post-it® notes are just paper and glue, but crafted in an innovative way for new uses. You innovate all the time. When traffic is blocked, you find another way. When obstacles appear, innovation begins.

There is a science to innovation. You can learn to become better at it. In this book, you will.

The world LOVES problem solvers, and you are one!

Networks multiply single units. A network of servers makes each connected computer more powerful than it was alone. A television network brings more entertainment and news resources than any station could acquire on its own. A group of people can multiply the power of each individual in it.

Margaret Meade is famous for saying, "What makes me think that a small group of people committed to a cause can change the world? Indeed, it is the only thing that ever has."

Each network starts with one person. You are that person. Connect with one, then another, and on until you have transformed your world!

Okay, Bambino, it is your turn to grow. Let Samara Beth be your guide. She's been there, too.

In the spirit of growth,

— **Jim Cathcart**

THE POWER OF SHOWING UP
HOW A FOREWORD FOUND ITS WAY HOME

- -

"I show up with courage. I stand out with authenticity. I ask with purpose. And I make a difference by being me."

Samara Beth

The ballroom lights of the Atlanta Convention Center glimmered across a sea of high heels and high hopes. It was 2006, and I was one of the top recruiters and an Advanced Director for *The Pampered Chef*, freshly crowned with ribbons and pins that sparkled under the stage lights. I had trained hundreds of women in breakout rooms, helping them build confidence and community through food, laughter, and leadership. But that day, I was the student—not the trainer.

Because *Jim Cathcart* was taking the stage.

He wasn't just a speaker; he was an energy field. His presence filled the room like a melody—calm yet commanding. His topic that day? *Relationship Selling.* A phrase that would rewire my understanding of business and, eventually, brand.

I'd been in events my whole life—corporate, social, nonprofit. I'd seen *everyone* on stage: Fortune 500 leaders, celebrity speakers, charismatic storytellers with perfect timing and million-dollar smiles. I was always the woman in black, headset on, clipboard in hand—the one *producing* the moment, not living in it.

But something about Jim was different. He didn't just talk about sales. He talked about *people.* About connection. About seeing every human interaction as an act of generosity—not persuasion. It wasn't about the close. It was about the *relationship.*

And when he said, "People don't buy because they're sold. They buy because they're understood," I felt it in my bones.

The session ended, applause erupted, and the crowd swarmed toward the exits. But I sprinted to the back of the ballroom— straight to the table where Jim stood signing books, CDs, and DVDs (yes, *CD-ROMs*—we're dating ourselves here).

"Hello, I am Samara Hurley," I said breathlessly, clutching my notebook and pen. "I don't know why, but something you said hit me hard. I've hired hundreds of speakers in my event career, but you... you spoke differently. You spoke to my heart, and all I have been training consultants on, but did not quite understand how to explain it as a business technique."

He smiled, signed my book, and wrote a message I still have today—right next to the still-shrink-wrapped CD-ROM. (I told him recently it's still in mint condition, and he laughed.)

That was the start of a connection that would take fifteen years to circle back—proving that when you plant seeds of authenticity, they bloom in divine timing.

FROM ATLANTA TO CLUBHOUSE

Fast-forward to 2020. The world had gone silent. Stages were dark. Ballrooms were empty. But on a social audio app called *Clubhouse*, the microphones came alive again.

Instead of conference rooms, we met in audio chat rooms. Entrepreneurs, speakers, coaches, and dreamers—all craving connection. It was there that Jim Cathcart's voice returned to my world like an old song on a new frequency.

I was in the middle of my divorce, rebuilding my business, my confidence, and my sense of identity. It was a fragile season, but it was also the birthplace of my next chapter. On those nights, surrounded by digital avatars and strangers who became family, I remembered who I was. I spoke. I coached. I contributed. I showed up. I got recognized.

One of those mentors—*Coach Ron Tunick*—noticed my energy and said, "You're like bamboo, Samara. You bend, but you never break."

And just like that, *Lil' Bamboo* was born.

The nickname spread across Clubhouse like wildfire—a symbol of my strength, grace, and resilience. And guess who heard it? Jim.

He laughed when I told him. "Lil' Bamboo," he said. "That fits you perfectly."

And then, just like that day in Atlanta years before, he reminded me that resilience and relationships are never random. They're earned through showing up—again and again —even when no one's watching.

THE ASK THAT CHANGED EVERYTHING

Months later, after countless rooms, conversations, and collaborations, I reached out to Jim with a trembling heart and a bold ask:

"Would you write the foreword to my book?"

It wasn't just about getting a name on a page. It was about honoring the connection that had inspired me when I was a young recruiter with big dreams and a headset full of ambition. He didn't hesitate.

"Of course I will," he said. "You've become exactly what you were meant to be—someone who inspires others to grow."

And then he gifted me something else—a phrase that now anchors my brand and my belief system:

"Samara Beth Hurley... Tomorrow is best early."

He said it to remind me—and now all of you—that the future doesn't just happen. It's *designed* by those who prepare, plan, and visualize it before anyone else sees it. That line now echoes across my speeches, my social media, my events, and even my heart. It's more than a quote. It's a calling.

LESSONS FROM THE FOREWORD

Jim Cathcart didn't just write the foreword to *WIN Your Brand: The Unapologetic Playbook for Becoming Iconic.*

He lived it—and reminded me to do the same.

Because success isn't about knowing the right people. It's about being *the kind of person worth knowing.*

It's about showing up before you're ready, standing out by being real, and asking—boldly—for what aligns with your purpose.

When I look back, the throughline is clear: 2006. 2020. Now.

Every time I've dared to *show up*, the universe has introduced me to the next version of myself.

And maybe that's the secret all along—relationships are not just the key to business. They're the blueprint for legacy.

BRAND SPOTLIGHT: RELATIONSHIP SELLING— THE FOREVER BRAND

The lights may fade after a keynote, the applause may quiet, and the slides may disappear from the screen—but the relationships you build in that room can echo for decades. That's what Jim Cathcart taught me. His philosophy of *Relationship Selling* wasn't about scripts, funnels, or closing ratios. It was about connection—real, human, lasting connection—and it forever changed the way I saw both business and branding.

Jim's message aligned perfectly with my *W.I.N. Framework.*

Because the truth is:

- **Willpower** helps you show up when no one else does.

- **Innovation** helps you stand out in a noisy world.

- **Networking**—the authentic kind—helps you stay connected when the lights go out and the market shifts.

That is *Relationship Selling.*

That is *Winning Your Brand.*

THE SENSES OF CONNECTION

- **Sight:** Eye contact across a table. A handwritten note in the mail. A speaker's smile that tells you they truly see you—not just your title or your wallet.

- **Sound:** The tone of a voice that says, "I believe in you." The way someone remembers your name at the next event. The sound of shared laughter that breaks down invisible walls.

- **Touch:** A firm handshake after a deal. A reassuring pat on the back. The electric moment of recognition when two people realize they can trust one another.

- **Smell:** Fresh coffee during a long conversation. The scent of hotel lobbies where ideas are born. The whiff of a brand-new book signed by the person who once inspired you.

- **Taste:** The bittersweet courage of asking for a collaboration. The celebratory sip after someone says yes. The satisfying taste of mutual respect—earned, not bought.

WHY RELATIONSHIPS ARE THE NEW MARKETING CURRENCY

In an age of algorithms, artificial intelligence, and endless automation, genuine relationships are the one thing technology can't replicate. Relationships are the new currency of business —and trust is its highest denomination.

When people feel *seen,* they stay.

When people feel *valued,* they refer.

When people feel *connected,* they buy—not just once, but for life.

It's not about selling *to* people anymore.

It's about building *with* them.

That's why my brand, *Samara Beth & Co.*, and my mission through *WIN Your Brand*™ are rooted in connection. Because brands don't go viral—*relationships* do. People share people they love, not products they're sold.

FULL CIRCLE: THE BAMBOO OF RELATIONSHIPS

Just like bamboo, relationships need time underground before they sprout. You can't rush trust. You nurture it—through consistency, communication, and care. Then, when the moment comes, growth happens seemingly overnight.

That's what happened between Jim Cathcart and me. One moment of connection in 2006. Years of quiet growth underground. Then, a forest of impact when he wrote the foreword to *WIN Your Brand*.

Relationships, like bamboo, bend with life's seasons but never truly break. They multiply—quietly, beautifully, and with purpose. They are the *forever brand*.

If you want to build a brand that lasts beyond the logo, build relationships that outlive the sale.

🔺 Coaching Tips:

1. **Be the First to Introduce Yourself.**
   Don't wait for permission to connect. The people who change your life are usually one bold hello away.

2. **Leave Every Room Better Than You Found It.**
   Whether it's a ballroom, a Zoom room, or a Clubhouse chat—your energy leaves an imprint. Be the light they remember.

3. **Ask. Always Ask.**
   The answer might be "yes," "not yet," or "not me"—but asking moves you closer to the right connection. Closed mouths don't create collaborations.

Reflection Questions:

1. When was the last time you introduced yourself to someone who intimidated or inspired you?

2. How can you bring your authentic energy into rooms—virtual or physical—so people *feel* your presence?

3. What opportunity might you be missing because you're afraid to ask?

SECTION 1

ROOTED IN CHALLENGE

· ·

THE EARLY YEARS, DISCOVERING IDENTITY,
& LEARNING TO GROW THROUGH LIFE'S
CHALLENGES

CHAPTER 1
LEARNING DIFFERENTLY, LIVING BOLDLY

- -

GROWING UP AS SAMARA BETH SCHWARTZ

I didn't know I was different… until someone told me I was.

At first glance, my life looked like the definition of normal. I was the youngest of three kids, the caboose in a family that was already moving fast. My mom was only nineteen when she married my dad, who was twenty-four, and together they built a life that, from the outside, appeared steady and grounded. My dad was the only one of three brothers to attend college, and he carried that determination with him all the way through the University of Maryland, where he earned both an undergraduate degree and a law degree. He was sharp, disciplined, and always seemed to know the right answer.

My mom, before she had us, was an X-ray technician—steady hands, precise eyes, caring in her own way. Once she became pregnant with my older brother, she stepped into the role of stay-at-home mom, a role she carried with devotion, voice, and exhaustion, raising three kids while my dad pursued his career as a lawyer.

My parents stayed married for over fifty-eight years. That's not a typo. Five decades plus of navigating each other's quirks, arguments, triumphs, and tragedies, until my father passed away at eighty years old. They were living proof that love, in its most enduring form, is not fireworks and fairy tales but steady commitment—a brand of loyalty I would cling to later when life tested me in ways I could not have imagined.

We grew up in Baltimore, Maryland, tucked into a neighborhood that felt safe and contained, like a bubble where kids could still be kids. The homes were small brick boxes, lined neatly side by side, with backyards just big enough for cookouts or slip-and-slides in the summer. Towering trees reached toward the sky, their branches forming a canopy that shielded us from the worst of the summer sun. Behind our house stretched a walking path that led straight to the elementary school—a literal trail toward my earliest classrooms—and beyond that were baseball fields, a huge playground, basketball courts, and the comforting hum of northeast neighborhood life.

My best friend lived directly across the street. We had known each other since we were two years old, which meant she was less a "friend" and more like an extension of myself. We knew each other's secrets before we could even spell the word "secret." Her front porch was as familiar as my own, and the sound of her screen door slamming and dog barking meant adventure was about to begin. Most of our circle of friends lived within walking distance, or at most a short bicycle ride away, with plastic streamers whipping in the wind.

Colonial Village in the '70s and '80s had a rhythm all its own. No driveways, no garages, just rows of cars hugging the curb on our narrow one-way street.

Snow days meant the muffled crunch of boots on packed ice as kids carried shovels house to house, hoping to make a few dollars clearing steps for neighbors. Summer evenings smelled of honeysuckle, the sticky sweetness floating through the air as I pedaled down the street on my Strawberry Shortcake two-wheeler, the plastic seat already faded from the sun. Sundown in the summer was spent chasing "lightning bugs" and putting them in jars. In the heat of summer, the community pool was our kingdom. The sharp scent of chlorine clung to our hair, and laughter bounced off the concrete walls. I worked there at a young age, my first taste of real responsibility, serving coddies —fried salted codfish patties slapped between saltines with a streak of yellow mustard—and snowballs dripping with neon-colored syrups, topped with marshmallow fluff that glued itself to your lips.

Autumn meant crackling leaves, raked into massive piles that invited a running start and a headlong dive. My neighbors would pay me to rake the leaves in their yards—another opportunity to make money to spend on *Fun Dip*® and *Fruit Stripe*® chewing gum, or a *Barbie*®.

Winter meant Fourth of July parades (in true Baltimore style, our seasons blurred, traditions overlapping), babysitting and dog-walking jobs, and the safe thrill of trick-or-treating when pillowcases sagged under the weight of candy. The streets smelled of fireplaces burning wood, and our breath puffed into the night like little ghosts as we ran from house to house. By the time we dragged our loot home, we could easily fill two pillowcases, and we spent the rest of the night sorting through chocolate bars, lollipops, and those tiny boxes of raisins nobody wanted. The holiday season brought neighbors together in the center, our community lighting massive Chanuka hanukiah (also known as menorah) candles and a thirty-foot decorated Christmas tree, celebrating multiple faiths side by side with potlucks, music, and laughter.

We thought we were lucky, and we were. We had cable television when some families still adjusted rabbit-ear antennas. We had a microwave when others waited for ovens to heat. We had good public schools within walking distance, road trips packed into station wagons up and down the East Coast, and summer camps that promised independence in upstate New York. What else could a kid possibly want?

I was the talker of the family, the one who filled silence with chatter, as if I were making up for lost time. Ironically, my parents thought I was mute until the age of two. The truth was, I simply didn't need words. I had two older brothers who anticipated my every gesture. I'd point, they'd deliver. Why talk when you've got minions? When I finally did open my mouth, words poured out like a dam breaking, and I haven't stopped since.

Being the youngest and only girl had its perks—more attention, more protection, more leeway. But it also came with pressure. My brothers stood at five-foot-eight and six-foot-two, towering over my eventual five-foot frame. From an early age, I learned that if I wanted to be heard, I had to speak louder, smile wider, and push harder. What I lacked in stature, I made up for in grit. But inside, I also knew something was different about me—not just my size, but the way my mind worked.

One brother had a photographic memory, the kind of mind that snapped up facts and filed them away neatly, like a library. The other had the body of an athlete and the brain of a scientist, thriving in labs and on fields. And then there was me. I worked harder than both of them combined just to keep up. I stayed up late, scribbling notes until the ink smudged across my hands, re-reading chapters until my eyes blurred. Still, tests came back with red marks that sliced my confidence.

By high school, the pattern was undeniable. This wasn't just a streak of bad grades. This was something bigger. Something that threatened to define me if I let it.

After more testing, the truth came out: I had a learning "disability"—though today it would be reframed as a "learning difference." My mind didn't process information in a straight line like the education system expected. It didn't march dutifully from A to B to C. It spun like a wheel, ideas orbiting around each other, connecting in creative webs that made sense to me but not to the bubble-sheet exams.

My doctor explained it like this:

"Unlike the traditional linear structure that standardized tests rely on, Samara's mind operates in a circular, holistic fashion. Imagine brainstorming with a topic at the center, surrounded by sub-topics, which in turn connect to more ideas—a dynamic web of thoughts rather than a straight line. It allows her to make creative, intuitive connections, but it also means she needs more time to organize her thoughts within the rigid formats required by standardized tests. She doesn't lack intelligence. She needs a different structure and pace."

It was both a relief and a gut punch. Relief that I wasn't broken. Gut punch because school wasn't going to bend for me.

In grade school, it meant hours of tutoring, index cards stacked high with vocabulary words, math drills whispered over dinner, and the sting of doing well on homework only to tank the test the next day. My brain lit up in discussions, my essays often earned praise, but the minute I was handed a multiple-choice sheet with tiny circles to fill in, my stomach dropped. The pencil felt like a weapon pointed at me, not a tool in my hand.

Standardized tests carried weight, and mine carried me down instead of up. Those scores followed me, determining placements, limiting opportunities. I realized early on I would have to build my worth elsewhere.

So I did. I poured myself into field hockey and lacrosse, where sweat equaled success. I worked nights and weekends, juggling jobs while classmates lounged. I volunteered, coordinated ski trips, joined prom committees, and filled every spare minute with activity. If my test scores said "average," my life said "extra." And socially, I bloomed. I floated between groups of friends, never belonging to just one circle, always connecting dots between people the way I connected dots in my mind.

The truth was, my learning difference was not a wall—it was a forge. Every time I hit resistance, I built something stronger inside of me. I was learning how to **live boldly** even as I was still learning differently.

MY SIXTEENTH BIRTHDAY SHOWDOWN

It was my sixteenth birthday when my mom took me to the Department of Motor Vehicles in Baltimore to apply for my driver's license. I can still feel the cheap plastic chair sticking to the back of my thighs as I sat waiting, my stomach in knots, my palms damp with teenage anticipation. Hours of practicing parallel parking in the narrow streets of Colonial Village, memorizing traffic signs, driver's education tutoring at the old church, and sitting tall in my mom's car driving in circles in parking lots had all led to this moment.

When I passed the test, the surge of victory felt like helium lifting me off the ground. I passed a multiple-choice and driving test! I floated through the building with a grin plastered across my face, my brand-new license clutched in my hand like a golden ticket. I remember staring at my photo—my awkward teenage smile, my permed hair just so—as though it were proof that freedom was finally mine. Sixteen. A license. The world was about to open up.

My mom had walked ahead and already started the car. I strolled behind her slowly, savoring the moment, holding my license at arm's length like a mirror, basking in the glow of possibility. The sun was bright, bouncing off the asphalt, and I could hear the faint sound of traffic humming in the distance.

And then—it all shattered.

A man's voice screamed. The crack of gunshots split the air, sharp and deafening. My body froze before my brain caught up. Instinct screamed louder than thought: *Duck. Run. Hide.*

I turned toward the DMV (Department of Motor Vehicles) building just in time to see the scene explode into chaos. An armored car sat parked at the curb, its steel sides gleaming like a fortress. Two security guards had their guns raised, their shouts piercing the parking lot. A robber—desperate, reckless—was trying to force his way into the cash-in-transit vehicle. The air smelled faintly of burnt rubber, as if the tires themselves recoiled from the violence. Time slowed, every sound amplified: The metallic click of triggers, the sharp pop of bullets ricocheting against pavement, the shrieks of bystanders ducking for cover.

I crouched low, my heart slamming against my ribs. My brand-new license was still in my hand, but its edges now cut into my palm as my fist clenched. Suddenly, over the chaos, another sound cut through—absurd, jarring, unforgettable.
Barbra Streisand. "What the...?"

From the cracked-open windows of my mom's idling car, her voice soared above the gunfire: *"Papa, can you hear me?"*

I wanted to scream and laugh at the same time. "Maaaaaaa! Duck! Turn that off! Gunshots!" But my mom couldn't hear me. The music was blaring, Streisand's plea from *Yentl* swelling with perfect irony as bullets echoed across the lot.

I sprinted toward her car, legs pumping, my lungs burning. The world tunneled down to one goal: to reach my mom. The asphalt radiated heat through my sneakers, and the smell of exhaust mixed with fear in the back of my throat. I dove into the passenger seat, slamming the door behind me, and shouted, "Shooting! Go! Go! Drive!"

At first, she thought I was exaggerating, being dramatic, maybe even joking. But then her eyes flicked to the side mirror. She saw the armored car, the guards, the robber, the raised guns. And in that instant, disbelief melted into panic. She floored it, pulling us out of the lot and onto the street.

Later that night, I sat glued to the television, my knees curled to my chest, watching the evening news. The anchors' voices were calm, detached, as they reported the attempted robbery. I searched the footage, hoping and half-dreading that I might spot myself—the terrified teenager clutching her brand-new license, sprinting like her life depended on it. Part of me wanted to be on camera. Part of me was just relieved to be alive.

And here's the truth: as terrifying as it was, I found the adrenaline rush fascinating. My hands still shook as I replayed the scene in my mind, but beneath the fear was a strange kind of awe. It felt like I had stumbled into a movie set, except this one didn't yell "cut." At sixteen, I thought it was a freak, once-in-a-lifetime experience. Little did I know that my life would feel like a movie for years to come—unscripted, unpredictable, and often far more dramatic than anything Hollywood could dream up.

Decades later, that song, that same song—"Papa Can You Hear Me"—I sang at my daddy's funeral service.

GET A JOB

The house rule was firm and non-negotiable: Once we turned sixteen, we had to get a "real job" to pay for gas in whatever used car was handed down to us. Babysitting wasn't steady enough, so I joined some of my friends at my first part-time salary job at The Bagel Shop.

The Bagel Shop was the place to go on the weekends, tucked in a shopping center with a jewelry store, a dry cleaner, and restaurants. It was the kind of place you'd miss if not for the constant stream of locals coming through its door. The smell hit you first—warm yeast, onions, and garlic toasting in the oven, with a hint of lox lingering in the air. The glass display cases were filled with baskets of golden, oversized bagels in multiple flavors that shone under fluorescent lights. The bakery case was filled with delicatessen cookies, brownies, rugelach, and fudge-topped yumminess.

While working there, I would run into neighbors, family, and friends, each one smiling as I handed them a paper bag with a bagel still steaming inside. It was comforting and familiar, and of course, I ate more than my fair share of bagels with cream cheese and lox. That salty, smoky salmon paired with the tang of vegetable cream cheese and the chew of a fresh, hot bagel felt like both a paycheck and a perk.

The owners were a married couple, weathered by years of poor decisions. They had the hollow-eyed look of people who had danced too long with drugs. At first, I tried to see past it—after all, a job was a job, and in the '80s, we didn't question authority figures the way we do now. But the husband, with his too-long stares and slimy comments, quickly became impossible to ignore. He was an inappropriate creep, and I learned to pivot away from his remarks, to dodge his presence, and to put up walls that girls my age shouldn't have to build. Back then, we didn't call it harassment. We just called it "gross" and got on with it. I walked away from slimy men before they could catch me in their web. That was my first quiet act of resilience.

Eventually, I left The Bagel Shop and found myself working at Windy Valley®, a Baltimore staple perched right off the Jones Falls Expressway and Joppa Road. If The Bagel Shop was about familiarity, Windy Valley was about nostalgia and spectacle. It was the kind of place that lived in people's memories long after they'd left.

The booths smelled of coffee so strong it could wake the dead. Grease from burgers and fries clung to the vinyl seats. Ice cream dripped down the wrists of children pressing their noses against the glass cases. The breakfast crowd ordered scrapple and eggs, the truckers leaned in for refills of bottomless mugs of coffee, and teenagers—awkward and hopeful—chose Windy Valley as a spot for first dates. Even my parents had once slid into those booths with ice cream cones in hand, decades earlier, when they were dating, long before I was born.

Windy Valley wasn't just a restaurant. It was a brand before we even used that word in daily life.

It had planted its roots in 1946, opening as a humble ice cream stand at the intersection of Falls and Joppa. The swirl of frozen custard cones drew families pulling off the expressway, while pony rides circled lazily nearby, a delight for restless kids. But its legacy went deeper: back in 1928, the Magdalena McCaffre family had begun acquiring farmland in Baltimore County, land that eventually gave way to Windy Family Farms, a tradition that still survives as a weekend escape and a testament to family legacy.

Decades later, fate folded in on itself in the most cinematic way. My best friend's grandfather—a man of grit and fortune—if I remember correctly, won the lottery and decided to buy Windy Valley. Imagine that: Winning a fortune and then turning around to purchase the very place that symbolized Baltimore family tradition. He modernized the space, brought Keno machines to the neighborhood, and stamped his own chapter into the ongoing story of Windy Valley. I always liked to imagine that he had bought the winning ticket there at the counter, as if destiny had reached out and rewarded him for his loyalty. That's what branding at its core really is—when a place becomes more than walls and windows, when it becomes memory, fate, and family history woven together.

At first, I thought working for him would be a step up from The Bagel Shop. But scooping ice cream was not the glamorous teenage job I imagined. The repetitive motion worsened the tendonitis in my right wrist, a nagging injury from field hockey. By lacrosse season, the pain was unbearable, each scoop like a reminder of what my body couldn't do. And then there was the other problem. The grandfather—my boss—had a way of lingering near me with comments that made my skin crawl. "If only you were eighteen," he'd mutter, as if my age were a countdown clock he was waiting to expire. *Grody my rody.* That was my reality: tendonitis in my wrist and innuendos in my ear.

But even in that mess, I learned. I learned how to speak with a bit of southern charm to swoon the truckers into leaving bigger tips. I learned how to dip frozen custard into hardening chocolate just long enough to create a perfect shell without losing the entire cone to the vat below. I learned about scrapple—a pork-based breakfast loaf made of trimmings, stock, cornmeal, and seasonings, fried crisp on the griddle. The smell of it—savory, salty, slightly metallic—filled the air every morning. Not my thing, but I quickly realized that scrapple, crab cakes, hard pretzels, and Utz™ potato chips weren't just food. They were Baltimore's food identity. They were symbols of heritage, shaped by Amish, Pennsylvania Dutch, and Chesapeake traditions.

And speaking of Utz chips—those were everywhere. Back then, Utz wasn't just a snack you grabbed absentmindedly. It was part of the sensory soundtrack of Baltimore. I can still hear the sharp crinkle of those red-and-white bags being ripped open in Windy Valley booths. The salty crunch paired perfectly with burgers, fries, and yet another cup of coffee poured from the bottomless pot. That's the power of immersive branding—when something so simple becomes forever tied to a time, a place, and the people you shared it with.

Eventually, I quit Windy Valley and took a quieter job as a barista and sandwich maker in a fancy French bakery. If Windy Valley was loud and gritty, the bakery was serene and refined. The smell of freshly baked baguettes filled the air, their golden crusts stacked in baskets along the counter. French music floated through the speakers instead of the clatter of greasy plates. Customers sipped cappuccinos in porcelain cups instead of slurping bottomless coffee from diner mugs.

There, I became a master of crafting cappuccinos with foam swirled and cinnamon garnish, of layering fromage and jambon (ham and cheese) on crisp, steamy baguettes until they looked like something out of a Parisian café. Before that job, I hadn't even known what "specialty coffee" was. And, being raised in a Jewish household, the only ham I touched was bacon on a hotel breakfast buffet. But this role expanded my palate, my awareness, and my sense of what a **brand experience** could be. It taught me that food could be not just sustenance, but theater. Not just product, but memory. And that lesson would serve me long after the smell of baguettes and sourdough had faded from my apron.

BRAND SPOTLIGHT: UTZ® POTATO CHIPS—A
CRUNCH THAT BUILT A CULTURE

If you grew up in Baltimore or anywhere in Maryland, Utz potato chips and pretzels weren't just snacks—they were part of your childhood soundtrack. The red-and-white bags with their simple block lettering, the smiling cartoon Utz girl with her bow and bobbed hair, the familiar salty crunch that seemed to echo in cafeterias, poolsides, and backyard barbecues—these were more than products. They were icons of belonging.

Open a bag of Utz and you didn't just get chips. You got the sound of summer, the taste of Little League games, the crinkle of wax paper lunches at school in The Muppets® lunchboxes. You tasted salt and vinegar, barbecue spice, or just the plain salted crisp that felt perfect alongside crab cakes, snowballs, or hamburgers hot off the grill.

Founded in 1921 in Hanover, Pennsylvania, Utz became a Mid-Atlantic institution, just an hour north of Baltimore. By the time I was growing up in the 1980s and '90s, Utz was everywhere: on diner counters, in brown-bag lunches, at crab feasts where Old Bay™ seasoned everything in sight, at lacrosse tailgates, and at sandy beach picnics in Ocean City, Maryland.

Utz wasn't a chip. It was a memory. I can still hear the sharp crackle of a bag being opened in the booths at Windy Valley, the chips passed around between burgers, fries, and cups of bottomless coffee. At birthday parties, kids would grab handfuls, salt dusting their fingers, and then dive right back into games of tag. That's the power of immersive branding: when a simple crunch ties your senses to a place, a moment, and a feeling so strong that decades later, one bite can transport you back in time.

Even today, Utz has managed to hold onto its authenticity while expanding nationwide. They remind us that brands that lean into roots and emotional connection create not just products but legacies. They create culture, one crunch at a time.

MOVING ON UP IN THE WORKFORCE

But Utz was just the beginning of my education in branding. My next lessons came wrapped not in chip bags, but in chocolate foil and the glittering shelves of Baltimore's first luxury grocery store.

My middle brother had landed a job as a waiter at a 1950s-style diner inside a brand-new gourmet supermarket that had become the crown jewel of a shopping center. The place felt like stepping into another universe: boutiques with crisp window displays, a Books-A-Million® with its own café, a TCBY® shop peddling frozen yogurt as the "healthy dessert of the future," a glittering custom jewelry store, and—most importantly—Sutton Place Gourmet®, Baltimore's first upscale grocery experience.

I followed suit and took a position as a chocolatier. My job required me to taste every truffle, every piece of marzipan, every chocolate-dipped fruit at least once so I could describe it to customers. Imagine being seventeen, standing behind gleaming glass cases piled high with glossy ganache domes and shimmering pralines, inhaling the rich, intoxicating perfume of cocoa and sugar. That was my daily reality.

We carried Joseph Schmidt® truffles—so indulgent they melted before you could even describe them. We stocked artisanal marzipan from Germany, France, and Spain, each piece shaped like miniature fruits, so delicate you almost felt guilty biting into them. Swiss chocolate bars wrapped in gold foil gleamed like treasure. Customers lingered over the counters as though they were selecting jewelry rather than candy. I quickly learned to spot the *shnorrs*—Yiddish for freeloaders—who circled the cases looking for free samples, and to distinguish them from the true buyers who savored every bite and returned with friends.

It didn't take long before my uniform waistband grew tighter. I indulged in the luxury I was surrounded by, sampling my way through more calories than I care to admit. Weight Watchers® soon followed. But so did wisdom: I learned that food wasn't just food. It was storytelling. It was branding. It was indulgence, memory, and aspiration all rolled into one bite.

And Sutton Place Gourmet wasn't just a candy counter. It was a temple to abundance.

Walking through that store was like walking through an atlas of flavors. Produce wasn't just stacked in piles—it was curated like art. Mushrooms displayed in baskets glistened with beads of mist: earthy porcini, delicate chanterelles, long-stemmed enoki that looked like tiny bouquets, and wild morels that seemed too exotic to even belong in Baltimore. Lettuces weren't just iceberg and romaine. There were over a dozen varieties—butter, oak leaf, frisée, endive—each crisp, fresh, and described in a way that made you feel like a connoisseur just for picking one. Cheese cases stretched for yards, with over four hundred varieties, their aromas mingling from tangy, sharp cheddar to pungent, blue-veined Roquefort. Oils and vinegars from around the world glistened under warm lights, their glass bottles catching the eye like jewels.

It was immersive branding before the phrase even existed—proof that a grocery store could tell a story of luxury, discovery, and belonging with every shelf.

When the store was acquired and renamed The Gourmet®, I shifted roles to cashier. Math wasn't my strength, but management had seen my work ethic and trusted me. To secure the role, I had to pass a test that required memorizing every single product code—and not just the numbers, but the names and appearances of every fruit and vegetable.

Talk about a Samara trigger moment. My palms sweated, my chest tightened, and I had flashbacks to fifth grade, where I once struggled to memorize rocks and minerals by color, shape, and property. Here I was again, surrounded by knowledge that seemed impossible to hold, yet required to master.

The store carried over seventy oils, four hundred cheeses, sixty vinegars, twenty-eight types of tomatoes, and twenty-five types of mushrooms. I had to learn them all. I had no idea there were fifteen types of lettuce! I studied furiously, repeating names until they rolled off my tongue, looking at the photos while tracing product codes until they embedded themselves into my memory. And I passed. I PASSED! That cashier job paid me nine dollars an hour—more than I had ever made before—and came with a deep sense of pride.

It also brought me into contact with Baltimore's Russian immigrant community. In the years following the fall of the Soviet Union, a wave of Russian families arrived in the city, many sponsored by local organizations. Their English was shaky at first, but their math was sharp, and they adapted quickly to the store's exotic food items. They became cashiers, stockers, and deli workers, their energy and eagerness unmistakable.

I loved working alongside them. I taught them English phrases and American customs. They taught me Russian words and stories of family, resilience, and rebuilding. My family had been Polish immigrants from Germany, after surviving the Holocaust, and I felt a kinship with these new arrivals who carried their heritage with them while carving out new identities in Baltimore.

In fact, my mom—an immigrant from Germany—partnered with a Russian man who had once served in the Soviet military. Together, they started a website-building business at a time when most people barely knew what the internet was. It was the mid-1990s, and the idea of a business existing online was revolutionary. That small spark of innovation would eventually lead me to meet my husband—but that's a story for another chapter.

THE POWER OF A BRAND

Looking back, I see that each job wasn't just about money for gas or a paycheck. Each job was teaching me the power of brand.

Utz taught me that simplicity and consistency build loyalty.

Sutton Place Gourmet taught me that abundance and sensory storytelling build aspiration.

And working side by side with new immigrants taught me that community and belonging are part of every brand that lasts.

These experiences shaped the way I would later see branding not just as marketing, but as identity. They were the foundation for my own reinventions—from psychology major to public relations student, from student leader to event planner, from "different learner" to bold brand-builder.

This was the beginning of my willpower. This was the beginning of faith in myself.

Coaching Tips:

1. **Your brain doesn't need to fit someone else's system.**
Lean into your natural strengths and seek environments where you can thrive, contribute, and actually feel good about yourself.

2. **Reinvention often begins with a pivot.**
Look for places where you can shift toward what feels aligned with your energy, creativity, and passion—even if it means taking an unconventional route.

3. **Determination beats memorization.**
Tools like teleprompters, slide presentations, or visual maps aren't weaknesses—they're strategies. Your path is yours to design, and how you deliver it is part of your brand. You may not be the only person in the room who needs those visuals and to use all senses to remember.

Reflection Questions:

1. **When have you been told you were "different" or "not enough"?**
    How did that shape the way you see yourself today?

2. **Where might a pivot serve you now?**
    What is one way you can reinvent your path this season so it feels more aligned with who you really are?

3. **What childhood memories shaped your brand identity?**
    How can you connect those early lessons to the story you're telling about yourself now?

Notes:

CHAPTER 2

FROM THE MARYLAND BUBBLE TO THE NEW YORK HUSTLE

I didn't just leave college—I left a bubble. A bubble of Baltimore bagels and sorority houses, crabcakes and college parties, snowball stands and late-night study sessions. In the spring of 1999, as my classmates were talking about graduate schools, first jobs, and moving back home, I was standing at the edge of something bigger. New York City. The BIG Apple. A place that promised both chaos and clarity and distance from my younger days.

But before I ever packed a suitcase for Manhattan, my life took a detour. One that started not in a boardroom, not at a networking event, but in the sanctuary of my synagogue on a cold November night.

A VOICE THAT SHOOK THE WALLS

It was November 1998. I was a senior at the University of Maryland, knee-deep in journalism classes, and my group had been assigned a class project on diversity. This was the '90s, remember—hardly anyone had computers with design or internet capabilities. In fact, only computer science and journalism majors had desktops in the classrooms that year. Lucky for me, my mom's business partner was a Russian immigrant who had pivoted from the military into one of the first website design companies in Baltimore. So, five of us college girls piled into my car and drove the forty-five minutes home for the weekend to build our project at my parents' house.

That Friday night, my mom insisted we join her and my dad at synagogue. The occasion? Our cantor—a world-renowned opera singer named Cantor Luterman—was celebrating his 25th anniversary at our synagogue (otherwise known as a Jewish temple). To honor our cantor, his best friend, the director of the U.S. Naval Academy Glee Club, brought the men's group to perform in multiple languages, including Hebrew. Tradition dictated they alternated every four years: sometimes the cantor would sing at the Naval Academy Chapel, sometimes the Glee Club would sing at Temple Oheb Shalom. This year, the Navy boys came to us.

We were fashionably late. A group of twenty-something college women who thought slipping into the back would go unnoticed. Instead, the ushers ushered us straight to the front row. Front and center. Right under the high bimah—the stage where the choir would stand, looming above us. Not exactly discreet.

And then they walked in. A line of midshipmen in dress navy blues, buttons gleaming under the sanctuary lights, shoes so polished they reflected the lights above. The air smelled faintly of wood polish and wax, and the quiet murmur of the congregation hushed to silence as the first notes rang out. They looked like something out of a movie. "An Officer and a Gentleman" meets "Top Gun" meets "Dead Poets Society." My friends and I giggled, elbowing one another like teenagers, each secretly claiming which one we thought was the cutest.

That's when I saw him.

Dark hair, clean-cut, with the kind of posture that made you believe discipline was carved into his bones. He had that Tom Cruise look, straight out of a prep-school film reel with thick dark hair parted down the middle and feathered to both sides. And he had something else—a gaze with green eyes. He looked at me. I looked away. I looked at him again. He looked away. A rhythm of curiosity, pulsing between music and silence.

THE PUNCHBOWL ENCOUNTER

The concert was a blur of soaring voices, harmony that rattled the stained glass, and the cantor's operatic range colliding with the Glee Club's powerful bass. The walls seemed to shake, the sound reverberating in my chest. By the time the last note faded into silence, I was flushed from more than just the music.

The midshipmen filed down the aisle, brushing past us in the front row. And there it was—a smile. Quick. Direct. Just enough to send heat rushing to my cheeks. His name tag read simply: M. Hurley.

Afterward, the reception buzzed with punch, petit fours, challah, and chatter. The air was thick with the smell of sweet kugel, rainbow and black-and-white cookies, rugelach, and overly sweet punch sweating in plastic cups. My girlfriends and I clustered in the corner, whispering and laughing about our front-row flirting, our voices rising above the scrape of chairs and bursts of laughter. That's when my dad noticed.

"What are you girls giggling about?" he asked, eyes narrowing in lawyerly curiosity.

"Your daughter thinks one of the midshipmen is cute," Rachel blurted out.

I froze. Please don't point.

"Which one?" my dad pressed.

And before I could stop her, Rachel pointed. "Back by the punch. M. Hurley is on his badge."

Shit.

Bright red, humiliated, I prayed my dad would chuckle and move on. Instead, he beelined across the room. My father, the lawyer who usually pushes us to leave so he can go to bed after events, the vice president of the synagogue board of directors, marched straight up to M. Hurley, shook his hand, and said, "Hi. I'm Michael Schwartz. I have someone you need to meet."

Next thing I knew, this dark-haired midshipman was walking toward me, guided by my very proud, very meddling father. My stomach was doing cartwheels. I might puke. Don't puke, Samara. Breathe.

"This is my daughter, Samara. She goes to the University of Maryland," Dad said.

Mike extended his hand. "Hi. I'm Mike Hurley. Nice to meet you. So…what do you uh…do?"

And for the first time in my life, I was speechless.

"Uh…I'm a senior at the University of Maryland."

He smiled. "Yeah, your dad just said that."

Mortified. Tongue-tied. My about-to-be former friends were staring, suppressing laughter. It was the first and only time in my life that I could not find words. Then, just like that, he was swept away by his fellow midshipmen, with their bus waiting outside for him, duty calling.

And he left without my number.

A WHITE PAGES LOVE STORY

What I didn't know was that back on that bus, Mike was telling his friends, "You're never going to believe whose dad introduced me to his daughter. The blonde in the front row." "Did you get her number?"

"Ah, shit. No."

For them, it was a game—how many numbers they could collect at concerts. Usually, at all-girls' colleges, not a room full of older congregants at a synagogue. But this one? This one lingered. Jewish or Christian, he couldn't shake the image of the girl in the front row. So, he did something outrageous.

He opened the Baltimore White Pages Phone Book and started cold-calling Michael Schwartzes.

"Do you have a daughter named Samara?"

Ten calls later, he realized Baltimore had way too many Schwartzes—ten pages front and back at the time. Eventually, he gave up. But fate wasn't done weaving us together.

ANNAPOLIS BARS, VALENTINE'S DAY

Fast forward to Valentine's Day, 1999. I was single at the time, spending the holiday with my sorority sisters in downtown

Annapolis—a strip of bars lining the marina, where midshipmen let loose on weekends, alumni frequent during sporting events, and tourists indulge in rich, creamy crab dip. The air smelled of salt water, fried seafood, and beer-soaked wood floors. We were just looking for fun, maybe a distraction from a holiday that seemed designed to rub loneliness in your face.

Half joking, half serious, several cocktails in, I asked around: "Anyone know a Mike Hurley?"

Most shrugged. Until Will.

Will lit up. "Yeah, he lives in my dorm."

What I didn't know then was that the Naval Academy only had one dorm. To me, coming from a university of 40,000 students, that seemed impossibly coincidental.

Will asked how I knew Mike, and I told him we met when they performed in Baltimore. I wasn't about to say it was The Glee Club at my synagogue—that didn't sound very "cool," and in the '90s most midshipmen had probably never even met a Jew. Many of them were from small towns, and even Mike only knew two Jewish people in his life before meeting me.

Let's just say Will had his eye on me, but when I pressed about Mike, he grew cagey. Still, word traveled fast. The next night, Mike heard about the blonde from Baltimore asking for him.

But out of loyalty, Will didn't hand over my email right away. He wanted his own chance.

Weeks later, right before my birthday, Will finally relented. "Here, she keeps asking about you anyway."

Mike emailed me: "Small world, isn't it?"

That email turned into hours-long phone calls, witty banter over AOL® dial-up (the screeching *eeee-errrrr-shhh-khhhhh* that made the whole sorority house know you were online), and eventually, a first date in April. By then, I had already been in New York for interviews with event legends like Richard Aaron, Jaclyn Bernstein, and Robert Hulsmeyer. I told myself Mike would just be a fling before I moved to the city to meet some Wall Street shark. I loved watching "Working Woman" and "Wall Street" before moving to the Big Apple.

But instead, I found myself living an "Officer and a Gentleman" moment. The kind of story you don't plan. The kind of story that plans for you, so you just go with it.

WHY THIS MATTERS FOR YOU

I share this story not just because it's romantic or cinematic. I share it because it's a perfect metaphor for what I teach in branding today. Life doesn't always give you a clear map. Sometimes it's embarrassing introductions, missed opportunities, dialing wrong numbers, and waiting months for the right timing. But when the brand—the essence—is strong enough, it pulls people back to you.

Mike didn't forget me after one smile in the front row. He searched. He followed the thread. That's what a powerful brand does—it lingers, it compels, it calls people back even when the details get messy. It takes more than one outreach to book a client. It averages twenty to thirty touches now in 2025. That number increases as the noise and distractions increase with technology and social media.

And for me, meeting Mike didn't just change my personal story. It taught me that resilience, serendipity, and showing up —even when you're tongue-tied—can set the stage for reinvention. Just like New York did. Just like life has done, again and again.

BRAND SPOTLIGHT: NEW YORK CITY—THE
BRAND OF AMBITION

In the late 1990s, New York wasn't just a city. It was a brand. A living, breathing, sensory overload that sold ambition like a commodity and packaged grit as glamour. You didn't just live in New York—you inhaled it, you wore it, you became it.

Fifth Avenue & Madison Avenue Luxury:

New York still belonged to the department store giants. Saks Fifth Avenue®, with its glowing holiday windows, Bergdorf Goodman® gleaming like a temple of couture, Bloomingdale's® with its "Big Brown Bag" swinging from every fashionable wrist. Madison Avenue pulsed with standalone boutiques: Chanel®, Hermès®, Prada®, Gucci®. Even if you couldn't afford to buy, you window-shopped, nose pressed to glass, letting possibility itself fuel your imagination. That was us. Mom always said, We can look, but we don't buy. Tiffany & Co.® glimmered with diamonds as you daydream of the days Audrey Hepburn filmed "Breakfast at Tiffany's" there and pray a handsome man offers you a Tiffany & Co.® diamond engagement ring, prior to registering as a couple for your China, crystal, and silver patterns in their luxurious showroom.

Central Park:

The lungs of the city—joggers circling the reservoir, horse-drawn carriages clopping down paths, kids chasing pigeons, and couples rowing boats under *Bow Bridge*. In fall, the trees turned amber and gold; in winter, snow blanketed the Great Lawn while skaters twirled at Wollman Rink®; in summer, Shakespeare in the Park® and music concerts reminded you that art could be both grand and free.

Downtown Flavor:

The Village buzzed with smoky comedy clubs, poetry cafés, drag queen bars, piano bars, and record shops. The Financial District pulsed with power brokers, oversized Blackberry® and Nextel® cellphones and walkie-talkies glued to ears, ticker tape parades, the smell of money, adrenaline dripping onto ancient cobblestones. Chinatown was alive with roasted ducks hanging in windows, knockoff bags and Rolex's® laid out on sidewalks, and the constant chatter of bargaining.

The mouthwatering smell of famous Jewish delis like Katz's® and Carnegie Deli® piled pastrami and corned beef high enough to feed two. At the same time, Sammy's Roumanian Steakhouse® turned dinner into a bar mitzvah nightclub, with sizzling garlic, vodka bottles encased in ice, business cards, and old photos attached to walls and ceiling. Everyone belting out "Hava Nagila" until their throats were raw.

The Nightlife:

By night, the city transformed into a playground. The

Meatpacking District was still rough around the edges, with underground clubs hidden behind unmarked doors. SoHo loft parties spilled champagne onto exposed brick floors. Uptown, jazz clubs hummed with saxophones and candlelight, while downtown, DJs mixed beats in warehouses that throbbed until sunrise. Every neighborhood had its own rhythm—salsa clubs in Spanish Harlem, reggae bars in Brooklyn, Irish pubs with sticky floors, and velvet-rope lounges where bouncers decided your fate with a glance. In the '90s, nightlife wasn't just about drinking. It was about being seen, being part of the pulse, and proving you could keep up with the city that never slept.

A World on a Plate:

In New York, food was a passport. Every block introduced you to another culture: dim sum in Chinatown, pierogis in the East Village, Dominican mofongo in Washington Heights, Greek souvlaki stands in Astoria, Italian cannoli in Little Italy, falafel in Midtown, Korean BBQ in Flushing, and Jewish bagels with shmear and lox everywhere in between. You could eat your way around the world without leaving Manhattan. Even the food carts told a story—hot pretzels, roasted chestnuts in winter, gyros wrapped in foil, and halal chicken over rice at 2 AM, with a line of club kids and Wall Street analysts waiting shoulder-to-shoulder.

Celebrities in the Wild:

New York's real magic was that the famous and the everyday coexisted without fanfare. One minute you were power-walking to a client meeting, the next Paul McCartney was seated at the next table at The Russian Tea Room® while your clients dined in private upstairs (true story!). Al Roker smiled and waved on a Today Show® set. Madonna might be slipping out the side door of a downtown club while you were hailing a cab. In New York, celebrities weren't on pedestals—they were part of the landscape. You didn't just read about them in magazines. You brushed past them on sidewalks, ordered lattes behind them at Dean & DeLuca®, or stood next to them at Broadway intermissions. Many times, you would see them as guests, performers, surprises, and clients at our events.

The Streets—Grit & Glamour:

Subways screamed and squealed under your feet, and you tried not to look at the rails to avoid seeing the massive rodents that live in the subway stations (I still have fears). Yellow taxis honked like a language all their own. There were no share-rides like Uber® or Lyft® back then. You hailed a cab in all weather, and you could go hours during a shift change during rush hour without one. The city smelled like roasted nuts, pizza grease, exhaust, and hot garbage—all mingling in the same humid summer air. Rain gave the streets a metallic tang, snow muffled the noise with slush swallowing heels and sneakers, while sunny days shimmered with heat waves rising from asphalt, and Mister Softee® trucks chimed in the streets.

Pop Culture Parallel:

If you want to know what it felt like to be young in New York in the late 90s, flip on *Friends*, *Seinfeld*, or *Sex and the City*. That was us. Cramped apartments with quirky roommates, breakups that felt like sitcom plots, late-night Chinese takeout in white cartons. Some nights we were Carrie Bradshaw with cosmos in hand, other nights we were Jerry and Elaine arguing over nothing in a diner booth. New York itself was the main character, and we were lucky to get recurring roles.

The Brand of New York:

What made New York unforgettable was its ability to brand ambition itself. It didn't matter if you were a twenty-three-year-old making $28,000 a year like me, or a Wall Street executive in a bespoke suit pulling in $200 thousand out of college. The city demanded everything—your hustle, your creativity, your resilience—and in return, it gave you stories that would last a lifetime. To survive New York was to absorb its brand. To thrive in New York was to become part of it.

For me, New York was my crucible. It was the stage where I learned that resilience and reinvention weren't buzzwords. They were survival skills. And as I set stages for clients across the city—from boardrooms to Broadway, rooftops to dinner yacht cruises—I realized that New York had set a stage for me too. It was teaching me to craft experiences that weren't just events. They were brands. And that lesson, I carry into everything I build today.

🔺 **Coaching Tips:**

1. **Every introduction holds a possibility.**
   You never know which "embarrassing" moment or random encounter will turn into a defining relationship. Show up, even when you feel tongue-tied.

2. **Connection beats perfection.**
   Branding yourself is not about flawless timing or smooth delivery—it's about being memorable, following up, and staying top of mind.

3. **Resilience creates opportunity.**
   From White Pages phone calls to New York hustle, success comes to those who keep looking for a way forward, even when the path isn't obvious.

☁ **Reflection Questions:**

1. **Where in your life have you mistaken an awkward moment for a failure?**
   Is it possible it could be the start of something bigger?

2. **Who in your orbit keeps coming back into your story?**
   It could be a client, colleague, or connection—and how can you nurture that relationship today?

3. **What "resourceful hustle" (like living off catered events or AOL emails) are you overlooking right now?**
   This could become part of your brand legacy later.

Notes:

CHAPTER 3
THE NAVY WIFE LIFE

WHAT DID I SIGN UP FOR?

You can plan a wedding. You can't plan a life at sea.

We had a stunning 200-person black-tie Jewish Navy wedding in Baltimore, Maryland, with friends and family witnessing choker whites and swords, military traditions, yarmulkes, and the traditional Hora dance. I was unaware that "I do" would quickly translate to "I'll do this without you for a while." First in submarine school with shift work schedules, living in Charleston, South Carolina.

Then, we moved to my parents' house in Maryland, until we moved to Groton, Connecticut, for submarine training.

On our three-month wedding anniversary in 2000, my new husband was stationed in submarine school in Groton, Connecticut, so my company in New York City put me up in hotels while I went back and forth. Except that the commuting didn't happen on my end with all the work required, and getting hit on at hotel bars got old fast.

[Enter my "Will and Grace" moment] My New York City employers let me sublet an apartment I found on the Upper East Side with a gay guy who was a personal trainer at a gym. I was so excited to have a "Will and Grace" roommate scenario. Still, he tore his rotator cuff, moved back in with his parents, and left me alone in our apartment with his grandmother's orange, brown, and yellow furniture and kitchenware. Total bummer.

I made the most of it, and my husband would stay with me when he could come down. Since I was planning to stay in hotels initially and had duffel bags of clothes, I just slept on an air mattress on the floor and used plastic storage containers. Most of my time was spent at the office and with the team anyway.

One night, I headed back to my apartment on the Upper East Side late, as usual, and realized that I had no clean sheets or towels, as they were at the laundry service. I would then take the subway train to The Plaza Hotel®—a five-star, world-renowned hotel across the street from Central Park —and be handed trash bags filled with a complete set of hotel logo-embroidered sheets, pillowcases, towels, a robe, and slippers. Royalty at its best.

After those three months, which seemed like forever, we moved to Amelia Island, Florida, where we built a house, because that's what you're supposed to do when you're first married and know you are going to move frequently. The house was behind schedule, so we rented an apartment for less than a year until it was ready to move in, and we loved our house and new neighborhood. It was our first time really living as a married couple. It seemed normal-ish. Except for one big thing...

My husband was deployed on a submarine, and I found myself living a double life: part full-time working, fast-lane New York City girl, part military wife, trying to navigate a world of rules, ranks, and relocations.

SEPTEMBER 11, 2001–WE REMEMBER

After living through a surreal few days on September 11, 2001, in New York City, watching the second plane fly into the World Trade Center Twin Towers, which I was just on a site tour with my clients two days prior. Ironically, at the same time, my husband's command was at the Pentagon for an Admiral tour, where ISIS terrorists crashed another plane. One could say that my priorities began to change after that traumatizing experience, followed by fearful months of deployment during a war that took the world by surprise, which was confusing and had Presidential quotas.

TRADING SUITS & *SEX IN THE CITY* STILETTOS FOR A CHEF'S APRON & SNEAKERS

Gone were the Manhattan clients and Manhattan martinis. I traded them for home shows and cooking demonstrations. I became an Independent Consultant with The Pampered Chef® —not because it was glamorous, but because it gave me purpose during long stretches of loneliness, blending in more with the military spouses and no more calls from my husband, while I was in New York City with clients.

I then relocated The Pampered Chef business from Florida to Hawaii, where we were stationed at Pearl Harbor on Oahu. Along with a six-week-old baby who rarely slept (he couldn't keep his food down), we had no furniture for months because it was on the slow boat from Florida. After living in a hotel for a while, we found a duplex in a neighborhood with all branches of the military and local Hawaiians. We built a wonderful community of friends and neighbors.

Besides the stunning scenery and weather, the silver lining of moving to Hawaii was that my business took off. I became a top recruiter for the company and the face of the leadership convention in Dallas. It was exhilarating. My team leaders joined me at conventions, and we built a solid team.

At a national Pampered Chef convention in Chicago, in the middle of a bustling convention center filled with thousands of consultants, I miscarried. Few knew, because I wasn't sure what was happening. I smiled through it. I worked through it. Cried in the convention center and hotel bathroom. I put my shoulders back and continued teaching my breakout room seminars to hundreds of consultants, and showed up for my team.

Then we returned to Houston. At that time, we left the Navy and went into the oil and gas industry. We lived in three different parts of the city and held different jobs.

The business and products taught me how to go from burning whatever I cooked to looking like a professional. It gave me income to pay for the extras we wanted in life. And it gave me an identity that the military spouses could relate to. I earned free incentive trips to Atlantis, Paradise Island, and luxury cruises. I was honored to win the Top Recruiter President's Award and became a celebrity within the community. The executive team had big plans for me, apparently. And, I met Jim Cathcart at a convention, and here he is two decades later, writing my foreword to this book.

BRAND SPOTLIGHT: U.S. NAVY

The U.S. Navy isn't just a branch of the military – it is one of the most powerful immersive brands in the world. Long before the word "branding" became popular in business circles, the Navy understood how to create an identity that moved people not just to sign up, but to serve with pride.

Think of the sensory branding:

The visual power of choker whites, dress blues, flags flying, and ships lined in formation.

The sounds of a military band, sonar pings, the crack of a ship's bell, or the "Anchors Aweigh" fight song echoing at graduations and games.

The smell of saltwater and diesel, embedding the idea of life at sea in the senses of both sailors and civilians.

The touch of pressed uniforms, the weight of medals pinned to a chest, the grip of a salute.

Even the taste of military life, from mess hall food to celebratory toasts on deck, becomes part of the collective memory.

Through its recruiting campaigns, the Navy has built stories that resonate emotionally across generations. From "It's Not Just a Job, It's an Adventure" in the 1980s, to "Accelerate Your

Life" and "Forged by the Sea," the messaging goes beyond words. These taglines evoke courage, camaraderie, travel, challenge, and belonging – all pillars of immersive branding.

Like any great brand, the Navy doesn't simply market what it does (sailing ships, deploying submarines, flying planes). It markets who you become when you're part of it, whether it be stronger, disciplined, global, or more resilient. The Navy's public relations efforts – air shows, fleet weeks, movies like "Top Gun" – immerse the public in the brand, sparking awe, pride, and sometimes envy.

For military spouses and families, the Navy brand creates another layer of identity: One tied to community, sacrifice, and resilience. It's not only the service member who wears the uniform – the entire family becomes part of the Navy's living story.

That's the mark of an immersive brand. It engages every sense, tells a story bigger than the individual, and creates a lifelong identity. Whether through a stirring anthem, a folded flag, or the sight of a ship sailing over the horizon, the Navy proves that brands built on emotion and ritual become unshakable legacies.

Coaching Tips:

1.   **Keep showing up.**
     Sometimes the bravest move is simply putting one foot in front of the other—even when your heart is breaking, your home feels empty, or your bank account is in the red.

2.   **Expect the unexpected.**
     Life will throw its own "deployments" and storms. Flexibility, community, and adaptability are the true hallmarks of resilience.

3.   **Be your own hero.**
     You do not have to be in the military, a doctor, a nurse, a police officer, or a firefighter to be considered a hero. In fact, some heroes are the ones who anonymously contribute to society. If you feel like no one is there for you, step up for yourself and find the right community. What are ten places you can look for everyday heroes to be a part of your life, if you find you may need help?

Reflection Questions:

1. **Where are you bending right now?**
    In what area of your life do you feel stretched thin, and how might that bending actually be building your strength?

2. **What does grace look like for you?**
    How can you offer yourself more compassion while still taking steps forward?

3. **Who is your support crew?**
    Which people, groups, or communities can you lean on when the storms hit?

Notes:

SECTION 2
BENDING, NOT BREAKING...
BARELY

MOM LIFE, MOVING OFTEN, STILL MANAGING
TO SERVE & SHINE

CHAPTER 4

MOM LIFE

There are moments in life where time feels like it both stands still and spins out of control. For me, one of those moments was hearing the words, "It's a boy!" A rush of warmth spread through me—the hum of the ultrasound machine, the cold gel still sticky on my skin, the smell of antiseptic lingering in the air, the beeping of machines. My heart leapt, already dreaming of blue blankets and baby giggles, while Gavin paces and contemplates whether he will share his LEGOs® with his baby brother.

And then everything shifted.

The nurse's footsteps hurried out of the room. "Wait, hold on, I'll be back."

I tried to remain calm as my son paced, still trying to decide which toys he would share with his unborn brother.

The nurse, my doctor, and the X-ray technician all came into the room this time. They reviewed the ultrasound and then said the words you do not want to hear next.

"Please meet the doctor in her office. The nurse is going to take your son to the other room to show him toys to play with."

The fluorescent lights buzzed louder, the walls closed tighter, and my joy collapsed into a heavy silence. I sat down in the chair across the desk from my doctor. Then the words came that cracked my world: "Your ultrasound is showing that your baby has a rare genetic defect called Omphalocele."

I had no idea what it meant—how to pronounce it, how to spell it, what the heck it was—but I felt the weight in my bones and the tears poured out while in shock. We called my husband and asked him to drive our son home since I could not stop bawling, and I drove my car home.

It was December, and the doctors were booked solid through the new year, with upcoming vacations, so we called a friend who was able to get us into his hospital the next week. Another example of it's who you know and who knows you.

WHAT LAMAZE CLASS DOES NOT PREPARE YOU FOR

Over the next eight weeks, my life became an endless cycle of waiting rooms and sterile corridors. The sharp scent of disinfectant clung to my clothes, the cool crinkle of exam table paper followed me from room to room, and the constant beeping of hospital monitors etched itself into my nerves. The doctors showed me three-dimensional ultrasounds: Cameron's tiny body with his liver, stomach, and intestines outside in a fragile sac. A hole in his heart. Only ten percent lung capacity.

Each fact and comment from doctors, nurses, friends, and family landed like a stone in my chest.

"He won't survive."

"If he does, it won't be a good life."

"He will never breathe without machines."

"He will require feeding tubes at home."

"He will require numerous surgeries as an infant and possibly growing up, if he lives that long."

"We can try this *Paint and Wait* procedure and put a fake belly button on him after we re-insert and move his organs around, but he will require way more surgeries. He requires more surgical procedures than any of the few Omphalocele kids we worked with in the past."

"We had one girl survive. She is five in this photo. But none of the rest survived either the pregnancy, or the birth, or the NICU."

"You will make your son autistic again."

"Cameron will have no life."

"You will have no life but taking care of your sick child."

"You should consider termination. They can do it at Planned Parenthood." "Wait…What?! Are you kidding me?"

"God only gives you what you can handle."

"I'm Catholic, and I am not sure what I would do if it were me."

"I'm Mormon, and I am glad to not be in your position, because I'm not sure what I would do."

THE WORST DECISIONS PEOPLE HAVE TO MAKE IN LIFE

I had previously miscarried at The Pampered Chef National Convention in Chicago, in the convention center and hotel bathroom, while thousands of consultants cheered outside. To finally be pregnant again had felt like hope. And now I was being asked to make a decision no mother should ever have to make—alone, exhausted, terrified.

And then came the coldest call of all—not from a doctor, but from hospital billing. No sympathy, no pause. Just numbers rattled off like a grocery receipt: "We spoke with your insurance company. Your son will reach his lifetime insurance maximum within eighteen months." As if my unborn child's life was already reduced to a balance sheet.

There was no manual for this. No pamphlet telling me how to walk out of a hospital with my heart shredded but my body still pregnant. No one told me how to keep breathing when hope was slipping through my fingers like sand.

I said it over and over to friends and family, like a mental case on repeat, "Cameron was diagnosed with Giant Omphalocele, a hole in his heart, and only ten percent lung capacity."

I wanted to keep him. I prayed, I fought, I searched for answers every day for eight weeks. My doctors, overwhelmed by the odds, gave me no hope. I was told that it was more a question of whether I want to deliver a stillborn baby now, or bury a baby a little later. And despite my heart's resistance, I did the one thing I didn't want to do. I wasn't alone, yet I felt alone, and it was killing me.

I went to the doctor's office alone this time. My husband had missed too much work for all the doctor's appointments leading up to this point, and he told me I had to go alone.

That day, I took a day off from my corporate event planning job. Yes, I was working my part-time job as the Director of Marketing for a corporate event planning and destination management company in Houston during all of this. My doctor administered a procedure while I cried hysterically and chattered my teeth to death. My hands were sweaty, my body felt like stone, and I was in shock. I fainted twice during the doctor's appointment. The nurse caught me by the head both times before I hit the floor. They put me on a cot, called the hospital and my husband, and they admitted me into the hospital. My best friend from the Navy flew in and held my hand the entire time. Bless you, Holly. It took me five days to deliver a stillborn baby that I had in my arms...lifeless, while I bawled for over three hours.

Without me realizing, since I was in shock and depression, my troops (non-military) gathered and planned Cameron's funeral with my clergy, informed everyone, and I just showed up. In the high-end luxury cemetery, where celebrities and wealthy Houstonians are buried, lies a tiny casket under where my husband's mother will one day be buried. My husband's family (particularly his aunt and uncle, grandmother, and mother) had plots within a brick entryway, and made a big deal over Cameron being buried in their plot. My husband's aunt and uncle made a generous donation to the cemetery and purchased a beautiful tombstone for Cameron, which we chose as the engraving.

We stood as a family, including our five-year-old son and my parents, who flew in the week they were moving from Baltimore to Scottsdale, Arizona, under a big white tent. Twenty-five of my friends from all parts of our lives and immediate family sat on organized chairs. My boss closed the office for the day, and all my co-workers attended, which was so thoughtful.

I tuned out as the words and blessings were said, and they lowered my angel into the ground. I looked up to see a sculpture of a little girl gone too soon, who is practically overlooking Cameron's grave. I knew that sweet butterfly-costumed angel would look out for my baby.

The funeral director did not charge us a dime, and he handed us our sign-in book, a memorial candle, and the collected condolence cards before the cemetery broke down the tent and chairs.

The entire week was a blur, but it broke me.

Of course, it didn't stop me from throwing Gavin his Transformers® bounce birthday party for sixty people that same weekend of the funeral.

It took a village to make that happen, but it was mostly planned since I was an event coordinator. My Mahjongg group brought a set to the hospital before they released me, and I assigned them tasks for the party favors, confirming the cake, carnival food, venue, and vendors, all while trying to focus on a Mah Jongg hand. It was a much-needed distraction, and I was never going to let this tragedy impact our son more than it already had.

Meanwhile, I was coordinating our company's marketing event at The House of Blues®. It was a huge success and a much-needed distraction from the sadness. It helps to love what I do.

We were an incredibly involved family. So, we were blessed with food deliveries galore, plants and flowers everywhere at the house, gift cards for restaurants, condolence cards, and casseroles in the freezer that lasted six months.

I wasn't just bending. I was almost breaking.

But I didn't. I kept moving. I kept mothering.

I picked myself up and I kept cooking, smiling, volunteering, running businesses, throwing marketing events at big venues, and showing up.

Because somewhere inside me, Lil' Bamboo was learning how to sway without snapping.

I wanted Cameron. I fought for him. I loved him. I lost him.

But I also had my superhero boy, Gavin. He needed me to be present, alive, functioning, and spoiling him for what he just went through—losing his brother and part of his mother. And I was barely doing that. Depression sat heavy in my chest, making even breathing feel like lifting weights.

Why did my favorite shows at the time, *Grey's Anatomy*, *Private Practice,* and *Scrubs* have to keep killing kids or making them sick on the shows? Everything triggered me.

When I buried Cameron in Houston, I buried a part of myself, too. The sound of dirt hitting the casket was louder than thunder. My arms ached with emptiness—the physical, primal ache only mothers know.

And then life threw another blow.

I was dropping Gavin off at my mother-in-law's after preschool on my way to a National Association of Catering and Events® (NACE) meeting. While swerving to avoid an erratic car, I slammed headfirst into a brick wall on a Houston highway. The screech of tires, the shattering of glass, and the acrid smell of smoke filled my world in seconds. My SUV crumpled, the transmission and hood scrunched into the windshield, the hot airbag punched me in the face, and my door jammed shut. Paramedics broke me free while hot smoke billowed from the hood. I passed out, but woke to the most beautiful sound in the world: Gavin crying in his car seat. Blood dripped from his bitten lip, but he was alive. My brave, little engineer was terrified, but he was alive. Thank God!

Even in chaos, I mothered. As the firefighters carried us to the ambulance, I told them to talk to Gavin about the gurneys, the hoses, the flashing lights—to explain the mechanics and calm his brilliant, overstimulated mind.

At the emergency room, a doctor asked me if I could be pregnant. I laughed through cracked lips. "Unlikely," I said, my voice flat, "I buried my son five months ago." I doubt my body would reproduce so quickly after all the trauma it endured. They made me take a test in the disgusting bathroom with blood on the floor and urine on the seat. I just wanted to take my boy home and forget the nightmare.

My husband was called and arrived at the ER, seeing my face black and blue from a combination of makeup, tears, blood, a broken nose, and despair.

The next day, while I was recovering, my husband went to the car tow yard to pick up my belongings from the SUV and assess the truck's condition. The tow yard employee offered his condolences, assuming the driver did not survive based on the condition of the Ford Explorer®. He told my husband that he has been in the tow truck business a long time, and has seen a lot of crushed cars, and this one was certainly a shocker that the driver was alive.

I was home recovering in bed the same night of the accident, and I went through three months of physical therapy. My neck pain never really went away, and I still have problems with my back and neck, but I never let that stop me.

All of this against the backdrop of Hurricane Ike recovery and a crumbling economy. Sirens outside, winds howling through broken trees, the smell of mildew from flooded homes. My own life mirrored the storm—bending in every direction, yet somehow still rooted.

Lil' Bamboo? Oh, she was tested, stretched, whipped around by every gust of wind. But she didn't break. By the grace of God or angels protecting her.

I pivoted.

I mothered.

I mourned.

I got back up.

We enrolled Gavin in kindergarten and updated our house to prepare for moving closer. My husband was still working full-time and living in hotels on weekends for his Executive MBA program. Due to the effects of the 2008 economic crash and Hurricane Ike, which impacted Houston in every way, I was laid off from my part-time job as Director of Marketing at a corporate event planning company and immediately started Celebrations By Samara LLC as a social event planning company. All I wanted to do was plan kids' themed birthday parties, weddings, and baby showers. Simple, short-term contracts, distraction from depression, while making money, so we could afford to move.

It was not an ideal economy for buying and selling a house at the same time. Plus, the area we were moving to, which would be closer to our son's private school, was more expensive. So, we would be downsizing to a smaller and much older house. I took it upon myself to start looking for houses near the school. It took longer than expected.

But weeks later, hope flickered again. A heartbeat on a screen. A whisper of new life.

"I'M PREGNANT!"

Whoa!

Not only am I pregnant, but based on the doctor's estimate, I was pregnant during the car crash.

"Shit! I had martinis the other night."

As my OBGYN would say, "Most women are drinking when they conceive anyway. Don't stress over that. Just don't drink now." That went without saying. But the worry and thoughts of possibly "killing" another baby, even if not intentional, sat heavily on the entire pregnancy, and I was nervous the entire time.

Every doctor's appointment. Every ultrasound. Butterflies in my stomach, sweaty palms, and clenched teeth.

As the pregnancy was showing quickly in my belly, which was not in shape yet from Cameron's pregnancy, we were scared to let people know this time that I was pregnant. After all, we recently had twenty-five people at our infant's burial.

As in my previous pregnancies, I was exhausted and started falling asleep at the wheel during the early-morning 60-minute commute to Gavin's school.

So, I staged our house, hired my friend to be our selling agent, who sold it in a week. The first family that saw it bought it.

DAMN GIRL! I was on fire!

It was time for a life and location change... Again.

Except we had a contract fall through and nowhere to move, so we moved into my husband's aunt and uncle's house for a few months, until we could close on a house for us.

HOMELESS & BUSINESS BUILDING

I remember being a guest in their mansion in Memorial Park while I drafted my first contract for a large social event my friend was insisting I produce. I had never produced a contract of that caliber, so I contacted my dear friend, who ran a successful wedding-planning company. She sent me a wedding contract as guidance, and I edited it to fit the type of religious event my client wanted me to plan. It's another example of making things work by "committing first and figuring out the rest later," as Grant Cardone would say.

Meanwhile, the house we were temporarily living in with our aunt and uncle was three stories high, in a gated community, with a stunning backyard featuring a large infinity pool and hot tub, a park behind the multiple-level patios, and sculptures everywhere. They traveled the globe and had artifacts from around the world in every room. It was like a museum. His uncle was chairman of a large oil company, and they had the life that my husband and I desired. If you are going to be homeless, this was certainly a great way to go instead.

I'll never forget being incredibly pregnant, taking a shower in their guest bathroom on the third floor, and the glass door of the stone shower would not open. I was stuck in the glass door shower, with no reachable towel, and no way to get anyone's attention. And for all I knew, our uncle was the only one home. And he was watching television on the first floor, which is also by the kitchen and master bedroom, so it would be unlikely that he would need to climb the stairs.

After banging, screaming, crying, and laughing, rinse and repeat, I gave up and lay on the wet, cold stone floor of the shower. Finally, I got back up and started screaming again. I was freezing cold and wet, but I did not want to miscarry, so the motivation was strong. All of a sudden, our uncle knocked on the door and asked if I was okay. I yelled that I was stuck in the shower and the door was jammed.

First, our uncle had to break into the bathroom. Then, I told him that I was naked with no towel, and that he would likely need a tool set. He shielded his eyes, reached around blindly for a towel, and threw it over the top crack of the door. Then, he was able to unscrew the hinges to release the door. We laughed so hard and could not wait for his wife and my husband to come home to share that story. It was one for the family books. I wanted to give up and be protective, but I also knew I had to keep going or I could be stuck in the bathroom for several more hours.

No matter what crap I am dealt, I always try to make it humorous in some way. Life is too hard as is, and I have my dad's sense of humor. So, go with it and make it a funny story later.

TIME TO MOVE… AGAIN

Finally, I found a house only six minutes from our son's school. We closed, moved in, and began to make the most of our new neighborhood, new school, and new house. And, preparing for our little girl.

That's right! It's a girl!!! So far, she was healthy, and I was on guard. Like paranoid on guard, but we had many ultrasounds and high-risk doctors, so we were in great hands. In fact, the same high-risk OBGYN who was helping us with Cameron worked with us for our next pregnancy. But, there was only one problem…

WAKE UP CALL

Before six in the morning, on a February weekday, Gavin

climbed into our bed. He made this a ritual every morning, but this time he said, "Mommy, you wet your bed!" I was in my third trimester, so I thought maybe my water broke, or hell, I could have peed in bed. I wouldn't put it past a pregnant woman who has been pregnant for years in a row.

I flung the sheets off to find blood everywhere. It looked like a murder scene, and I was in panic mode while trying to keep Gavin calm and pack a hospital bag at the same time. We tried calling every friend we could to drop Gavin off on the way to the hospital so they could take him to school, but most phones were silenced at that early hour. Finally, one family answered, and we dropped him off and went right to St. Luke's Hospital in the Houston Medical Center.

Same hospital, same nurses, same floor, same Valentine's Day decorations, same anxiety, sweat, and tears, exactly a year later from when I held my stillborn baby in my arms for over three hours. I was beyond triggered, and the doctor was not ready for my daughter to come out. In fact, she was at a conference in Florida that week and wanted to see if we could delay the birth as long as possible for my baby to develop her lungs more and for my doctor to return. I was a high-risk case, and having a stranger deliver my daughter was not my preference, given all I went through exactly a year before.

Oh, wait, plus, my husband was in midterms at his MBA program, and the professors made it clear that no excuses were tolerated for missing midterms. One of his professors allowed him to make it up, and we ended up having to schedule my cesarean surgery around his midterms. It was laughable because our daughter was ready, whether we were or not.

Then came Ava. My surprise. My rainbow. Born premature, underweight, lungs not fully developed, yet screaming with lungs that declared: "You're still alive, Mommy. Keep going."

And through it all, I learned what true willpower + faith in my God really means. My higher power has a plan, whether I want to agree with it or not.

The joke is on me, because my kids' birthdays are February 13th, 15th, and 19th. With Valentine's Day in between, every year has been an emotional roller coaster of joy, love, loss, depression, and pride, triggered every time the stores started putting Valentine's Day cards, gifts, and candy out. Earlier and earlier every year. Those bastards. That used to set me off like a water hose for a good week or two.

But then, I saw the benefit of having pastel pink, purple, and green chocolates and decorations on sale for Ava's birthday parties every year. So, there you go. Always looking for that silver lining, especially when Mama Bear owned an event planning business and went all out for her kids' birthday parties.

It should be noted that my son, Gavin, was not happy that his mom was in the hospital, not just one year, but two consecutive years, the week of his birthday parties. Of course, the show went on with the help of my girlfriends and vendors because I stopped at nothing and created a village.

SO, WHAT, SAMARA?

You may ask, "Samara, so what? Who cares about your life story and your kids? Many people have stories of pregnancies and family and stuff."

It's the million-dollar question: Why do I share some of my personal stories in a book about how to *WIN Your Brand*?

Why am I telling you all this story in a book about branding and business?

Because our personal brand is born in the fires of our lived experience.

My brand isn't built on glossy perfection. It's built on resilience, on bending without breaking, on learning to mother while grieving, and on rebuilding when the walls of life crash down. Those lessons—in the hospital room, at the cemetery, in the wreckage of a totaled car—taught me the same principles I coach my clients with today:

- Show up even when it hurts.

- Lead with purpose, even in storms.

- Know that bending is surviving—and resilience is your brand.

This is why I can look my clients in the eye and tell them, "You can WIN Your Brand. You can build something extraordinary from the hardest seasons of your life. Because I've lived it, and there's even more to come. And I know you can, too."

Like I always say, "The best time to build a brand is when you are rock bottom and the economy is crappy, because you can only go up!"

BRAND SPOTLIGHT: NEW MOTHERHOOD

Motherhood is not marketed with billboards or jingles, but it is one of the most recognizable brands on Earth. The "brand of Mom" is built through immersion of the senses and emotions:

1.   **Sound:** The sound of a newborn's first cry or the silence of grief after loss.

2.   **Touch:** The touch of tiny fingers gripping yours, or the weight of a casket far too small.

3.   **Scent:** The scent of baby powder on a rainbow child, mingled with hospital antiseptic.

4.   **Sight:** The sight of stretch marks, car seats, strollers, and sleepless eyes reflected in a mirror.

5.   **Taste:** The taste of tears in the middle of the night— sometimes of joy, sometimes of sorrow, sometimes of exhaustion.

6.   **Intuition:** The sixth sense of a mother. Something only a mother can know or understand.

Motherhood brands itself not through slogans, but through legacy and resilience. Every diaper bag, every milestone photo, every casserole left by a neighbor after a loss becomes part of the brand story. Hospitals, insurance systems, and even children's diagnoses shape the backdrop, but the core brand promise of motherhood is always the same: *you will bend, but you will not break.*

In marketing terms, the Navy recruits with power, Utz with nostalgia, and luxury stores with exclusivity. Motherhood recruits with love—irrational, unconditional, sometimes painful, mostly exhausting, always binding. It is an immersive brand that requires every part of you—body, mind, and soul— and in return, it carves out strength you didn't know you had. Love you didn't know you could feel unconditionally.

For me, burying Cameron almost broke me, but it also branded me forever as a mother who could carry grief in one hand and Gavin's autism diagnosis in the other. And when Ava's lungs screamed at her premature birth, the brand of motherhood reintroduced itself: You are still here. Keep going, mama! You got this!

That's the power of the Motherhood brand: It forges resilience out of heartbreak, bends but does not snap, and leaves every mother with a mark—not of perfection, but of presence. It's a "branding" in the heart, instead of a tattoo on the skin.

🔺 Coaching Tips:

1. **Grieve & grow at the same time.**
   Grief has no timeline. You're allowed to mourn while still moving forward. And remember—it's never your place to tell someone else when they should "get over it."

2. **Bending is not breaking.**
   When life stretches you in every direction—through loss, diagnoses, or sleepless nights—remember that bending is surviving. Strength is born in flexibility.

3. **Your worth is unshakable.**
   Even the hardest choices, even the seasons of exhaustion or heartbreak, do not define your worth as a parent, a partner, or a person. Love and resilience do.

Reflection Questions:

1. **What felt like it broke you**—but actually built your strength?

2. **Where in your story can you offer yourself more compassion and forgiveness**?

3. **Who or what is your "miracle child" right now**—that reminder that life still has more in store for you?

Notes:

CHAPTER 5

CELEBRATIONS AMIDST CRISIS

YOU CAN ONLY GO UP

When people talk about success stories, they love the part where someone "starts a business in a recession." It sounds noble. Glamorous. Ballsy.

For me, it wasn't a headline. It was survival.

It was 2009. The smell of mildew still lingered in Houston from Hurricane Ike's devastation, the economy was crumbling, and my body was still healing from pregnancies, loss, and the crash. I was grieving Cameron, raising Gavin, and navigating Ava's premature beginnings. My world was a carousel of doctor appointments, school drop-offs, therapy sessions, sleepless nights, and expenses higher than income.

Starting a business wasn't glamorous. It was a lifeline.

I launched *Celebrations By Samara LLC.* in Houston, not because the timing was perfect, but because it was the only way forward. I had a gift. I had experience. I had connections. I had community. And I had a fire in my belly that whispered: *You are not done.*

BUILDING JOY IN THE MIDST OF GRIEF

I started small—balloons and birthday parties. Kids' celebrations, where sticky fingers reached for candy, parents sipped coffee (or wine and beer) while chatting, and the laughter of children filled backyards and community centers. I wanted to bring joy back into my home, even if I couldn't bring Cameron back.

I wasn't just planning parties. I was planning healing.

Even the dads who usually hovered awkwardly in the corners of bounce houses or buried themselves in their phones came alive at my events. Because I didn't just feed the kids' needs—I fed the parents' souls, too. I created spaces where everyone felt included. Pizza boxes mingled with gourmet platters, paper plates sat beside cocktail glasses, and parents who normally dreaded kids' parties lingered until the very end, and booked me for theirs as soon as they could.

Celebrations became therapy. Each balloon I tied, each cake I sliced, each detail I obsessed over was a way of pushing forward. A way of saying, *"Life is still here. Keep living it."*

THE B'NEI MITZVAH THAT CHANGED EVERYTHING

One morning, in the hum of Panera Bread with the scent of bagels and coffee wafting through the air, I was sitting with my Mah Jongg group when my friend leaned across the table. Her twins were about to turn thirteen.

"I want you to plan my twins' B'nei Mitzvah," Marlene stated without really asking.

I laughed. Shook my head. "No, thank you, I'm sticking to birthdays and showers. Something small. Something light."

But she didn't take no for an answer.

For weeks, we went back and forth. Marlene's voice persisted. My resistance was stubborn. Until finally, I said yes.

The theme was Cirque, and it was spectacular and a massive challenge from day one. She was an interior designer and wanted to host the big event at the interior designer mall, in the foyer, inner mall areas, and the restaurant. A year of restaurant owner and mall drama led to a magnificent event. The spaces shimmered with vibrant colors, LED rainbow light changing and reflecting off the acrylic square tables for twelve throughout the room, acrobats twirled overhead, and kids danced on top of dance cubes on a branded dance floor, holding branded party favors and fun LED swag, while parents toasted with themed and branded cocktails. The music thumped, the buffet lines buzzed, and in every corner, joy pulsed like electricity.

And just like that, my phone started buzzing. Guests lined up, asking, "Can you do my daughter's bat mitzvah? My son's bar mitzvah? Our school gala? Our company holiday party?"

That one "yes" transformed my business. I averaged three to five bookings per event, and after three years, Celebrations By Samara was booked two years in advance.

Within three years, Celebrations By Samara was ranked among the top event planning companies in Houston. My company was in the *Houston Business Journal.* My face was on the covers of glossy magazines in gyms, community centers, private schools, and doctors' offices. I was quoted in newspapers, interviewed on ESPN Radio, and photographed in the society section of Modern Luxury soirées.

My events weren't just parties—they were productions. Galas with champagne towers that sparkled like chandeliers. Corporate events with stages that pulsed under spotlights. Surprise birthday parties with bands, branded dance floors, premium open bars, and activation stations. Mitzvahs where kids felt like rockstars, and parents entertained friends and clients.

The hum of society galas, the clinking of glasses at volunteer events, the applause at industry award shows—those became the soundtracks of my success.

But behind the curtains, I was still grieving. Still carrying the weight of loss. Still raising a child with special needs. Still navigating a marriage that was fraying under the strain.

Celebrations became both my brand and my coping mechanism.

And then came the moves. Next, Vancouver, British Columbia. Five years later, to Scottsdale, Arizona. Each time, I packed up my life, uprooted my family, and rebuilt the business from scratch. New vendors, new clients, new culture. Reinvent, rebrand, rebuild. Rinse and repeat.

WHEN THE MUSIC STOPPED

Then came COVID. The pandemic did more than shut down our country. It shut down the entire world.

The silence was deafening.

No cocktail chatter. No DJ booths thumping. No floral centerpieces filling the ballrooms with fragrance. Just the echo of cancellations, the ping of contracts dissolving in my inbox, and the crushing weight of refunding every last client.

Celebrations By Samara went into the red. My bank account mocked me with negative balances. PPP loans were denied because we moved from Canada to the United States in December 2019. Unemployment didn't come. For the first time in decades, there were no stages to set. No events to host. No girlfriend meet-ups. No carpools. No friends. We had just moved to Arizona for the first time, so we were starting at new schools, and I was hired to plan a non-profit gala that took place on March 6, 2020, in Scottsdale. Once that was over, the contract ended. My business was about to take off, but then nothing happened anymore.

It was devastating.

But it was also divine.

It didn't happen overnight. There are many things that occurred, businesses and a non-profit that were started, evolved, and then shut down due to personal reasons.

However, years later, out of the ashes of Celebrations By Samara came the birth of something even more aligned: **Samara Beth & Co.** A brand not just about parties, but about immersive branding. About helping visionaries create legacies that outlast a ballroom. About using my story—the grief, the grit, the glory—to build something bigger.

That's not just reinvention. That's innovation.

You will have to read on to hear all about the Celebration of what's to come…

BRAND SPOTLIGHT: CELEBRATIONS AS A BRAND

Celebrations are more than parties. They are **sensory experiences that brand our memories.**

- **Sight:** Balloons cascading from ceilings, candle flames flickering, gowns shimmering under chandeliers, crystals catching light on centerpieces, the flash of the photo booth camera lights.

- **Sound:** Laughter echoing across dance floors, the crackle of sparklers, DJs dropping beats that shake the floor, the beat of the drum of the band, young children running and giggling.

- **Smell:** Buttercream frosting mingling with champagne bubbles, flowers perfuming banquet halls, smoke machines filling stages with mystery.

- **Taste:** Sweet challah at mitzvahs, elegant hors d'oeuvres passed on silver trays, birthday cake melting on a child's tongue, rich chocolate fountain as a newly married couple dips a strawberry for each to taste.

- **Touch:** Satin table linens, cold champagne glasses, the warm hug of friends who haven't seen each other in years, sweaty professional dancers leading the line dances on the dance floor.

Great brands, like great celebrations, understand this truth: **people don't just remember what happened—they remember how it made them feel.**

For me, Celebrations By Samara became more than an event business. It became a reminder that even amidst grief and chaos, joy can be created. It became proof that resilience can be branded. And when COVID shut it down, the brand didn't die—it evolved.

That's what lasting brands do. They transform.

Coaching Tips:

1. **Release to reinvent.**
    Every ending makes space for the next beginning. Don't cling to a version of yourself or your business that no longer serves you.

2. **Evolve as you evolve.**
    Your brand, like your life, is allowed to grow and shift. Pivoting isn't failure—it's strategy.

3. **Start over with experience.**
    A fresh start backed by wisdom is far more powerful than a naïve beginning.

Reflection Questions:

1. What identity, title, or business are you holding onto that may no longer serve your next season?

2. How can you honor what you've built—even if it's time to release it?

3. What's something new you feel called to launch or explore right now?

Notes:

SECTION 3
NURTURING LIL' BAMBOO

"EVERY HALLMARK MOVIE HAS A BOTTOM
OF THE BARREL."
MY DAD

CHAPTER 6

MY HALLMARK™ MOVIE

There are moments in life where the universe scrapes you bare, empties your pockets of hope, and leaves you at the bottom of the barrel—fingernails clawing at the sides, desperate to find even one reason to keep going.

That's where I was when my twenty-two-year marriage shattered. My identity as a Navy wife, an oil expat spouse, and a woman who had built a life around someone else's journey was ripped away in one sharp motion. Divorce isn't just losing a partner. It's the unraveling of an entire belief system: the family dinners, the traditions, the vacations, the joint friend groups, the rituals you thought would carry you into old age. Every box in a moving truck wasn't just furniture—it was the sound of laughter, tears, and love you thought would echo forever, packed into silence.

And just as I was crawling out of that wreckage, I lost my Daddy.

DADDY'S GIRL

He was my rock. My believer. The one who reminded me that grit and stubborn strength weren't flaws—they were lifelines. He understood entrepreneurship, the suffocating weight of credit card debt, and what it meant to start from scratch. He understood being one of three kids, carving your way through life with little more than determination and silly humor, something few could get away with repeating over and over and over again for decades.

I was his youngest. His only daughter. His "Sugar Snackers."

He kept every keepsake, drawing, clay sculpture made by us and my kids in his office for decades. He was that dad and that poppy. The one who cherished every accomplishment of his family, large or small.

Even in my forties, I'd curl into his lap, my arms wrapping around his neck as if time had never passed. His pointer finger would hook into my petite hand as we walked along the Atlantic City or Ocean City boardwalk, salty air brushing our faces, funnel cake powdered sugar sticking to our fingers. We stuffed blue cheese into Costco olives, sipped martinis and old-fashioneds with extra cherries for me, watched explosions of light on the movie screen during action flicks, and belly-laughed until tears streaked our cheeks at the silliest things. Sneaking ice cream or pizza in with several reminders, "Don't tell mom [or Bubbye if it was my kids] that we spoiled dinner" to nights at the driving range learning golf. Even at eighty years old, my dad would do cannonballs off the diving board into the pool, throw us all around in the water. He never acted his age, unless in lawyer mode, and that is what we all loved about my dad.

That's who I lost when cancer came. What went from bladder cancer pronounced likely gone after five sessions of chemotherapy led to a stroke the night he about to watch a *Hallmark* movie with my mom, to a helicopter ride from one hospital to another, to recovery and therapy, to being able to sing "Happy Birthday" to my mom, to being told to go home and do outpatient rehab to the shocking and abrupt news that daddy had pancreatic, liver, lung, bladder cancer, to my mom telling me they were going home that night for hospice at home, to bringing him to hospice facility after being at home was a nightmare, to passing away later that week.

It devoured him. One minute, he was my jokester, my lawyer, my anchor. The next, he was breathless in a hospice bed, his skin cool beneath my cheek, a single tear caught in the corner of his eye that would never fall, wrapped in my arms and the blanket my daughter and I made him.

OUR HALLMARK TRADITION

If you've ever watched a *Hallmark* movie, you know: it's predictable. A small town. A love story. A happy ending. My parents lived for those films. After fifty-eight years together, they curled into the couch each night, remote in hand, watching couples find love under Christmas lights, cowboy ranches, or summer fairs. It was their nightly ritual, their way to balance the heaviness of world news and my father's litigator law career.

When my kids and I visited, we joined them. It became a family activity. Anytime a couple kissed, we'd yell, "Hallmark Kiss!" And just when things hit their darkest moment, my dad would grin and say, "Bottom of the barrel," counting down the minutes until the turnaround. He had it down to the minutes before the end of the movie.

It was corny. It was comforting. It was ours.

So, when he died, I thought: *This is it. This is my bottom of the barrel.*

GRIEVING IN SILENCE

But even then, I stayed strong. For my kids. For my mom. For everyone else near and far. I kept posting updates on Facebook until my fifteen-year-old "OG" account was hacked and stolen from me—another piece of connection ripped away when I needed it most.

I broke down in closets, in cars, in bathrooms. But publicly, I was strong.

And oh, how I can still hear his voice on the other end of the line:

"You can do anything you want. You are stronger than any challenge. Look at what you've overcome. You wouldn't be happy if you weren't working toward something big. It's who you are. You're my Sugar Snackers, and I love you."

Sugar Snackers—not just a nickname. A superhero cape. A brand of resilience I didn't choose, but one I inherited.

I laid in the hospice bed with him long after his breath was gone, long after his body grew still. Hours passed before they wheeled him to the morgue. I pressed my face against his shoulder, inhaling the fading scent of aftershave mixed with hospital antiseptic, trying to memorize it before it slipped away forever.

THE GRAVEYARD OF GRIEF

Three months later, on Cameron's birthday, I brought a lawn chair to my father's unmarked grave. I carried Cameron's blanket, nightie, hospital bracelet, photos, funeral memorial candle, and the box of hospital angel keepsakes. I laid them out across the patchy grass, dirt still raw beneath my fingers, and for the first time in fourteen years, I didn't mourn my son.

I mourned my Daddy.

The grief I had kept hidden to hold everyone else together finally poured out. Sobs that shook my chest. Yells that cracked my throat raw. Whispers that begged him to take care of Cameron in heaven.

And he visited me. I felt him. In dreams. In signs. In the hush of the night, when I swore I heard him chuckle at one of his own old jokes. Sometimes I cried, missing him. Sometimes I cursed him for leaving us. Always, I carried him.

BADASS BAMBOO EMERGES

Life didn't let up. Jobs were lost. Clients canceled. Bank accounts were negative. Credit cards maxed out. My body bore bruises of stress, anxiety, and depression. But I refused to stay crumpled in the dark too long. I had mascara-streaked days where false lashes slipped down my cheek—but I got up. I had sarcastic laughs in the middle of breakdowns—but I kept moving.

That's how **Badass Bamboo** was born.

Not perfect. Not polished. But unbreakable.
I rose with grit. With humor. With hustle. With the audacity to say: *I will not stay curled up in grief. I will rise—even if I have to do it in stilettos.*

And now, my purpose is clear.

To help others build their stages, their brands, their legacies.

To take everything trauma tried to steal from me and turn it into light.

Into resilience.

Into a call to rise higher than we ever imagined.

THE HALLMARK™ RITUAL

Hallmark doesn't just sell cards or movies. It sells certainty in an uncertain world. It delivers a ritual: a guarantee that no matter how bleak the headlines or heavy your personal life, you can count on hope being restored in the final scene. *Hallmark* can also guarantee there will be "Christmas in July," with continuous uplifting stories of hope, giving back, and joy throughout the year.

From a branding perspective, *Hallmark* is a master class in immersive consistency. Everything it touches—movies, cards, ornaments, stores—tells the same story: *love, belonging, nostalgia, and hope.* It is less about innovation and more about emotional dependability. And that has made *Hallmark* not just a brand, but a cultural anchor.

MY HALLMARK™ COLLEGE JOB

What I did not mention earlier was that my job while in college was at *Paperworks Balloons and Gifts,* right in College Park at The University of Maryland. It was founded by an entrepreneurial teenager who grew to be a successful and amazing woman. I still see her when she visits Arizona. Her store was filled with Hallmark and other greeting card brands, balloons, gifts, Beanie Babies™, and corporate gift baskets we created.

At that job, I learned how to blow up and tie balloons properly (it's an art form most do incorrectly), how to make gift bags, boxes, and baskets, how to use the sales register, and organize Hallmark and American Greeting cards, stationery, and more holiday decor and gifts than you can imagine. I had the joy of selling the college athletic "celebrities" roses and gifts to them for their Valentine each year. That was way more fun than the long line of grandmothers and mothers waiting in line outside our door, starting at four in the morning for the release of new Beanie Babies.™

Paperworks Balloons and Gifts was the perfect college job for me because I was able to sell, create, and erect balloon arches and columns, as well as decorative centerpieces, for private off-campus events across Maryland and Washington, DC, and on the university campus. It was the start of my balloon and corporate gift basket experience, and I learned how to drive a delivery van to drop off gifts to make people smile. I continued to use those skills up until today.

HALLMARK™ IN OUR HOME

For me, *Hallmark* will always be tied to my parents. To yelling, "Hallmark Kiss!" across the living room with my kids. To my dad's perfectly timed prediction of the "bottom of the barrel" moment before the happy ending. Watching him and my mom hold hands, night after night, as the magic unfolded on screen. *Hallmark* became part of our family's language, our inside jokes, our rhythm. And after his passing, it became a thread of memory, healing, and presence. It became my mom's evening activity alone after my dad passed, and it brings her comfort.

That's the proof of an immersive brand: when a product transcends what it sells and embeds itself into your family story. When it becomes shorthand for comfort, tradition, and even resilience.

And here's the parallel: **my brand is built on the same promise.**

Just like a *Hallmark* movie, my coaching meets people at their "bottom of the barrel"—the messy middle of grief, reinvention, fear, or failure. I don't sugarcoat the pain. I sit with them in it. But I also hold the lantern that says, "This isn't the ending."

With W.I.N.—Willpower, Innovation, and Networking—I guide them toward their final scene: the one where hope shows back up, reinvention is possible, and resilience takes center stage, ultimately landing them on all the stages they need to succeed in their personal and business dreams.

Hallmark guarantees happy endings on screen. (Keep your head out of the gutter on this. Hahaha!) I guarantee something even more powerful: the tools to create your own happy ending in real life. Because unlike the movies, you don't just watch the story play out—you get to rewrite it.

✦ BRAND SPOTLIGHT: HALLMARK™ ✦

Hallmark™ is more than greeting cards and cozy movies. It is a brand of comfort and predictability—a cultural promise that no matter how messy the middle gets, the ending will hold hope. That is why it has lasted for generations, spanning holidays, seasons, and entire family traditions.

Think of how Hallmark saturates the senses:

- **Sight:** Snow-dusted small towns, glowing Christmas trees, candlelit living rooms, and couples finally locking eyes as if the whole world has been waiting for them to get it right. The golden light, the softened edges, the look that says, *peace is possible.*

- **Sound:** Warm piano chords, swelling orchestras, laughter around dinner tables, predictable dialogue that soothes like a lullaby. The rhythm itself becomes reassurance: tension, conflict, misunderstanding, reconciliation.

- **Touch:** Fuzzy blankets draped across couches, mugs warm in hand, tissues ready for tears of joy. It is mittens brushing together, boots crunching on fresh snow, and finally—the embrace of reconciliation.

- **Taste:** Hot cocoa topped with whipped cream, gingerbread cookies dusted with sugar, popcorn during movie marathons, martinis or glasses of wine as girlfriends or sisters catch up at the kitchen table. Simple holiday flavors elevated to symbols of belonging.

- **Smell:** Pine-scented candles, fireplaces crackling, cinnamon rolls baking, cocoa steam rising in winter air. Scents that don't just fill a room, but anchor memories.

🎄 Coaching Tips:

1. **Your "bottom of the barrel" isn't the end.**
   Like a *Hallmark* script, it's the turning point. Even when life strips you bare, it can still flip toward hope.

2. **Carry legacy forward.**
   The people you lose can still shape how you live, how you lead, how you brand. Your story is their story, continued.

3. **Resilience is messy, not pretty.**
   It can come with mascara streaks, cracked voices, and broken hearts. But showing up anyway? That's where the magic is.

Reflection Questions:

1.   What has been your "bottom of the barrel" moment, and how did it shape you?

2.   Whose voice do you still carry with you—and how does it guide your choices today?

3.   If your life were a *Hallmark* script, what would your next "scene of hope" look like? I bet you will have fun with that one ;)

Notes:

CHAPTER 7

THE BADASS BAMBOO THEORY: YOU DON'T BOUNCE BACK, YOU BOUNCE FORWARD

A NICKNAME THAT BECAME A LEGACY

The first time I heard the words "Lil' Bamboo," I was sitting on a nasty, used donated couch by a new apartment neighbor, with my laptop on an Amazon box used as a coffee table, during the still evolving COVID-19 pandemic, donated coffee cup in hand, made from a donated coffee machine, providing free value to an international community through the Clubhouse™ social audio app.

For years, I allowed the noise of experts, new audio app friends I never met before in person, and mentors from my past to distract me from the fear, stress, and anxiety of my future and current situation. My world at the time felt like it was crumbling—divorce dragging out, the events business shut down, no access to my belongings, working part-time to work around my kids' schools and therapy. My identity shaken, trying to keep my head above water.

And then came Coach Ron Tunick, his booming radio voice filling the speakers of my iPhone like he was speaking directly to my soul.

"Samara, you are one of the most interesting and smartest women I know. You're like bamboo," he said without hesitation. "Lil' Bamboo. That's you." Coach Tunick knew I was only five feet tall and had a petite frame from our FaceTimes.

At first, I laughed. A plant? That's my nickname now? But then I sat with it. His words rang louder than the noise of my self-doubt. Bamboo bends but doesn't break. Bamboo survives storms and grows stronger after every cut. Bamboo is one of the fastest-growing plants on Earth, spreading quietly underground before shooting toward the sky.

"Lil' Bamboo," he repeated, his voice the kind that could sell out stadiums or calm a crowded boardroom. "That's who you are."

Coach was determined to have me start a podcast with other co-founders of our networking group, but I was not quite as confident as he was that Lil' Bamboo was the nickname that would become my business brand.

COACH RON: THE WHALE HUNTER

To understand why those words mattered so much, you have to know who Coach Ron Tunick was to me.

174

Coach wasn't just another business coach. He was a force of nature. A man who had lived several lives—banker, broadcaster, radio host, entrepreneur, and mentor to thousands. He taught people how to land "whales," his term for the big opportunities in business and in life.

When Coach spoke, you listened. His California golf humor mixed with hard-hitting truth, I always picture him with his cigar and scotch in hand on his patio. He didn't sugarcoat and was definitely "old-fashioned" and offensive to some at times, but he always left you feeling like you were capable of more than you imagined.

I remember one call where I was in tears about everything falling apart—events canceled at my job after people ran out of PPO (government funding) and businesses were laying people off, our events space was a construction site and weddings were getting smaller as costs for food, beverages and event glass increased dramatically, therefore company holiday parties turned into employee bonus checks and social events became DIY (do it yourself) craft parties, which impacted my sales targets set by the owners of the venue. While my bills were piling up, my kids watched me try to hold it together with duct tape and coffee, and my parents seemed exhausted by my situation. Coach didn't let me wallow.

"Lil' Bamboo," he said, "you don't bounce back. You bounce forward. Trust me. I see something in you that you do not see in yourself yet."

The line hit me like lightning. Up until then, I'd been obsessed with "getting back" to where I was before—before divorce, before I had no house, before grief, before COVID destroyed my events business. But Coach's wisdom flipped the script. Why would I want to go back? Back was gone. Forward was where life was waiting.

Coach's style was simple yet profound. He taught me, and everyone he worked with, that managing emotions was everything. "Most people sabotage their day in the first five minutes," he'd say. "Pause. Breathe. Wait three days before reacting. You'll see things differently."

According to Coach Ron, "You can change your life in one minute, by changing your thoughts by going to a bookstore, and buying a book like 'Think and Grow Rich,' by Napoleon Hill... buy a book and take personal responsibility for your life and actions."

Fortunately, I own multiple copies of "Think and Grow Rich," autographed by Sharon Lechter and Russell Brunson. The Napoleon Hill Foundation has been a wonderful inspiration and education for me as an entrepreneur. I am blessed to have personally met, and spoken on stages with legends, like David Meltzer (Chairman of Napoleon Hill Institute), global icons such as Brian Tracy, Jim Cathcart (author of my foreword to my book), Les Brown, Jack Canfield, Mark Victor Hansen, Loral Langmeier, Lisa Nichols and others from the movies, "The Secret" and "Think and Grow Rich."

In fact, many successful people, like Mark Victor Hansen, co-founder of "Chicken Soup for the Soul," once told me that he read "Think and Grow Rich" every day when he needed guidance and strength, at his rock bottom, living out of his car and trying to figure life out.

According to Coach Ron, many of us sabotage our day right from the start by letting our emotions run wild. He teaches that "managing the highs and lows of our physical, mental, and emotional state is critical. The most successful people, what he calls the 'whales,' master their emotions by pausing."

Coach Ron Tunick reminded me that the people who succeed aren't always the smartest or richest. They're the ones who keep standing up, even after the storm knocks them flat.

In the words of Napoleon Hill in *Think and Grow Rich*:

"Every adversity, every failure, every heartbreak, carries with it the seed of an equal or greater benefit."

That seed? That's bamboo. It's resilience. It's growth that pushes not backward into what was, but forward into what's possible.

BAMBOO: NATURE'S BLUEPRINT FOR RESILIENCE

The more I thought about Coach Ron's nickname, the more I studied bamboo itself. And I realized nature had handed us the perfect blueprint for resilience.

Bamboo doesn't rush. For years, it builds an invisible root system underground, stretching farther and deeper, unseen. Then, when it's ready, it shoots up overnight, sometimes several feet in a single day. People call it "sudden success," but the truth is, bamboo has been working the whole time, unseen, building the foundation it needs to grow tall.

Bamboo bends in storms. Typhoons can knock down giant oaks, but bamboo sways gracefully, only to stand tall again once the winds die down.

Bamboo grows through concrete. Have you ever seen a tiny green shoot break through a sidewalk crack? That's bamboo. Resilient. Persistent. Unstoppable.

Bamboo multiplies. When nurtured, it spreads, creating entire forests where once there was only one stalk.

And isn't that life? We spend years building underground—skills, networks, faith—before the world ever notices us. We survive storms by bending when we want to break. We push through impossible obstacles. We grow into communities, families, movements.

At that moment, I realized it wasn't just a nickname. It was a prophecy.

MY BAMBOO PARALLELS

When I look back, bamboo was woven through my life long before Coach Ron ever said the word.

Losing Cameron nearly broke me. But like bamboo, I bent in the storm and grew roots in faith and resilience.

Building Celebrations By Samara during a recession wasn't about bouncing back to my old career. It was about bouncing forward into a business I never thought possible.

Divorce after twenty-two years could have left me shattered. Instead, it pushed me to rise into Badass Bamboo, a woman who no longer defined herself by someone else's story.

Moving 30 times, across homes, cities, and even countries, could have scattered me. Instead, each move was a new shoot of bamboo breaking through concrete, proving I could grow anywhere.

Like bamboo, my strength wasn't in standing rigid. It was bending, swaying, and springing forward after every storm.

BRAND SPOTLIGHT: BAMBOO

Bamboo isn't just a plant. It's a *brand*—an immersive experience recognized across the globe.

- **Sight:** Sleek bamboo flooring, towering stalks in meditation gardens, chopsticks set across steaming bowls of ramen. Bamboo charger plates under elegant china at an exclusive luxury event, bright with cherry blossoms, bamboo stalks, and hanging lanterns.

- **Sound:** The hollow knock of bamboo flutes, the rustle of stalks swaying in the wind, the calming tap of a bamboo fountain in a zen garden.

- **Touch:** Smooth bamboo utensils, woven baskets, the cool strength of bamboo furniture. The smooth leaves I touch and groom after watering each week. The softness of a cuddly panda bear on a bamboo stalk.

- **Taste:** Bamboo shoots in stir-fry, bamboo tea, the earthy tang of food served in bamboo steamers.

- **Smell:** Fresh greenery after rain in a bamboo forest, subtle woody notes in incense, the clean scent of bamboo sheets.

Bamboo has branded itself as the universal symbol of resilience, sustainability, and balance. Cultures around the world—from Asia to South America—have tied bamboo to strength, prosperity, and longevity.

For me, bamboo became more than a material or a metaphor. It became my mirror. My reminder that even when I feel fragile, my roots run deep. My growth is inevitable. My story is not over.

THE RALLYING CRY: THE BADASS BAMBOO THEORY

Here's what I know now:

You don't bounce back. You bounce forward.

Life is not about clawing your way back to who you used to be. It's about transforming into someone stronger, wiser, and more alive than before.

Do you think I don't have days when I feel like I am falling five steps backward after two steps forward? Of course I do. I didn't say it was easy. I never said I don't have hours when I just want to disappear with no noise or light, except for nature.

Bamboo doesn't apologize for bending. It doesn't cling to the old storm. It rises into the sun, multiplies, and creates entire forests from a single stalk.

That's the invitation of the **Badass Bamboo Theory**—to see yourself not as broken, but as growing. To see every setback not as an ending, but as a rerouting. To choose forward momentum over nostalgia.

And this is why it connects directly to **WIN Your Brand**. Just like people, brands don't survive by staying rigid or trying to "go back" to the way things were. They thrive by adapting, by innovating, by bending without breaking, by rooting deep and multiplying their reach.

You are bamboo. Your brand is bamboo. And together, you can bend, sway, and rise higher than ever before.

🔺 **Coaching Tips:**

1.   **Nurture your roots.** Success takes time underground. Build your foundation—skills, networks, faith—before expecting visible results.

2.   **Practice flexibility.** Storms will come. Instead of resisting, ask yourself: *Where can I bend without breaking?*

3.   **Bounce forward, not back.** Setbacks aren't invitations to return to "before." They are springboards into something greater.

4.   **Pause before reacting.** As Coach Ron taught: take three days before responding to big emotions. Clarity comes with space.

5.   **Multiply your growth.** Don't just grow for yourself. Spread your strength into your community, your family, your brand.

Reflection Questions:

1. Where in your life are you trying to "bounce back" instead of choosing to bounce forward?

2. What underground "roots" have you been building that no one can see yet?

3. How can you apply the Badass Bamboo Theory to your brand—bending, adapting, and thriving in ways that create legacy?

Notes:

CHAPTER 8

THE LAST GALA

THE NIGHT THE MUSIC PAUSED

The ballroom shimmered with golden uplighting, a thousand flickers of reflection bouncing off crystal glassware and polished silver. The smell of fresh roses mixed with the faint tang of hotel carpet cleaner, the kind that lingers even under layers of perfume and champagne bubbles. Servers glided through the aisles in crisp white shirts and black aprons, balancing trays of hors d'oeuvres—mini crab cakes with aioli, seared beef skewers, and cucumber bites with dill cream.

Three hundred fifty guests filed into the tented pavilion, laughter rising in waves, punctuated by the clinking of wine glasses and the hum of conversation. The energy was electric, celebratory, and yet—beneath it all—there was an undercurrent. A murmur about something spreading overseas. A hesitation in a handshake. A bottle of hand sanitizer tucked at the edge of the silent auction table.

I stood at the back of the ballroom, headset in place, clipboard in hand, heels clicking against the floor as I darted between AV cues and catering questions. Joshua Malina, our celebrity keynote, stood ready in the wings, a mix of charisma and ease, his smile lighting up the stage before he even spoke a word. My team hustled like clockwork—lighting cues fired, the screens glowed with campaign graphics, the band hit their opening notes.

And then there were the handwashing stations.

Ugly gray plastic things meant for carnivals and county fairs. I had fought for them in the days before the event, insisting they be delivered, even when my boss rolled his eyes and called them "an eyesore." Hilton ended up footing the bill. I didn't care if they clashed with cocktail dresses and tuxedos. Guests were eating, shaking hands, hugging, and fist-bumping. Something in my gut told me we couldn't ignore the whispers about this "virus." Practical over pretty—that was my call. And looking back, those stations may have been lifesavers.

From the stage, the sound of applause swelled. Joshua Malina leaned into the microphone, delivering a keynote that had people leaning forward in their seats, laughing, nodding, pausing to reflect. The spotlight glowed on his face, the audience bathed in the warm embrace of unity, purpose, and philanthropy.

It was everything an event producer dreams of. Oversold despite cancellations. Guests buzzing with joy. A night where the world outside the ballroom—at least for a few hours—didn't matter.

Except it did.

As I stood there, scanning the room, I had the eerie sense that this was it. The last gala. The final symphony before the silence.

Within days, the same hands that clinked champagne glasses were hoarding toilet paper from Costco. The same laughter-filled tables dissolved into Zoom squares and lonely living rooms. The ballrooms went dark. And my industry—the very heartbeat of my life—flatlined overnight.

That night wasn't just another gala. It was the end of an era.

BRAND SPOTLIGHT:
GALAS AS CULTURAL BRANDS

Galas are more than fundraisers. They are sensory theaters, designed to immerse attendees in a brand's values, vision, and mission.

- **Sight**: Ballrooms glowing with uplighting, guests in black tie, silent auction tables shimmering with promise.

- **Sound**: Champagne corks popping, applause thundering, keynote voices stirring hearts.

- **Smell**: Roses, perfume, hotel polish, warm bread carried by waiters.

- **Touch**: The smooth program booklet, the cool stem of a wine glass, a handshake sealing a donation pledge.

- **Taste**: Perfectly plated entrees, desserts shaped like art, cocktails named after the cause.

A gala brands more than an organization—it brands hope itself. It tells donors and attendees: *You are part of something bigger. You belong to this moment.*

The pandemic reminded us how fragile this cultural brand is. It's not just about tables and tickets. It's about community and connection. When the world lost galas, we lost more than events. We lost a ritual of togetherness.

🔺 Coaching Tips:

1. **Design for Immersion**: Every event, whether 30 people or 300, should engage all five senses. That's how you make it unforgettable.

2. **Prioritize Safety Over Perfection**: Sometimes the "eye sore" is the lifesaver. Your brand is built not just on beauty, but on trust.

3. **Anticipate the Future**: Great leaders listen to their gut and prepare for storms others don't yet see.

4. **Anchor the Emotion**: Don't just focus on logistics— ask, *What do I want people to feel when they walk away?*

🌣 Reflection Questions:

1. **Think about the last "gala" in your own life—a season, project, or relationship that felt like a triumphant ending. How did you know it was closing?**

2. **Where can you prioritize safety and trust in your brand, even if it doesn't look glamorous at the**

moment?

3.   **What rituals or gatherings in your life are part of your brand of hope? How can you protect and reimagine them?**

Notes:

CHAPTER 9

CHAOS IS COMPOST

. . . .

WHEN THE WORLD WENT SILENT

The ballroom lights faded. The applause from that last gala still echoed in my ears as I drove home, heels kicked off in the passenger seat, my phone buzzing with both praise and compliments for a job well done, but also news alerts I didn't yet want to believe. Something was shifting. I could feel it. But I couldn't imagine how quickly the shift would become a landslide.

Days later, my calendar dissolved. Back-to-back events that had once packed my weeks—galas, mitzvahs, corporate holiday parties—were replaced with cancellations. At first, the calls were polite: *"We'll postpone to summer."* Then came the panic: *"We have to pull the plug."* Finally, the silence: unanswered emails, locked venues, empty inboxes.

The once-booming heartbeat of my industry stopped cold.

At home, chaos reigned. Four of us crammed into a three-bedroom apartment in Scottsdale. My son was pacing with his headphones, trying to make sense of virtual school. Gavin actually made the hilarious comment, "I have been training my whole life for this. Staying home, not socializing, or not going to school. This is fantastic!" He did feel that way for a while, until it got old. Really, really old.

My daughter sat cross-legged on her bed, laptop propped on pillows, teachers flickering in and out on Zoom, and no one had online etiquette or knew what to do.

My husband camped at the tiny dining table with a desk instead of a family table, desktop, muting calls so he wouldn't hear me clattering pans in the kitchen five feet away. And me—feeding everyone, soothing meltdowns, trying to salvage a business while the news played like background static. I spent most of my time in my bedroom to stay out of everyone else's way.

Fear smelled like bleach. Lysol™ wipes and toilet paper became currency. The sharp sting of hand sanitizer filled the air, burning the cracks of our already raw skin. The grocery store shelves were stripped bare: toilet paper, paper towels, and tissues were gone; aisles were empty, pasta and canned goods vanished, and Clorox™ and bleach were like gold. I can still remember the hollowness of pushing a cart past rows of picked-clean shelves, the sound of wheels squeaking on linoleum, the tension in the air thick as strangers avoided eye contact.

Talk to no one. Wear your mask. Make sure you have a special virus mask. Wear gloves. Touch only what you buy. Clean what you buy. Clean your car and counters after you buy. And, if delivered, clean everything well before putting it away.

Clean your phone, glasses, AirPods, car keys, and hands over and over and over again.

It was an OCD (obsessive-compulsive disorder) crisis for everyone.

Pure insanity!

Outside, streets were eerie and silent. No honking. No rush-hour lines. No clinking of silverware from restaurants. Just the sound of sirens in the distance, the occasional barking of a neighbor's dog, and the echo of our own isolation.

And yet—there was creativity. Families chalking rainbows on sidewalks. Neighbors clapping from balconies to thank first responders. Birthday parades with honking cars and balloons taped to windows. And on screens everywhere: Zoom happy hours, Facebook Lives, Instagram cooking demos, religious services streamed from living rooms. Technology became both our lifeline and our prison. Much of the technology was a silver lining that still exists because of the pandemic.

I felt the loneliness settle heavy on my chest. The absence of hugs. The aching silence of my phone that once rang with client calls and new friends in our new city. Nights where anxiety pressed down so hard. The bars in homes went from happy hour to earlier hour. People were drinking, many were doing drugs, and others were worse.

And yet, compost.

It didn't look like it then, but the decay became fertilizer. Out of chaos, small seeds broke through.

It was born from compost. From loss, grief, and collapse. From the ashes of canceled galas and silent ballrooms.

The world was unraveling: ships stranded at ports, goods stuck on containers, restaurants shuttered, people dying alone in hospital rooms without family by their sides. But amid the mourning, there was something else too: rebirth. Small businesses pivoting to mask-making, distilleries producing hand sanitizer, teachers reimagining classrooms online, and entire industries discovering Zoom, Slack, and AI like they were newly minted inventions.

Yes, there was a loss. There was fear. There was death. I lost a friend. And some of my friends still suffer from the virus and vaccines. But there was also resilience, reinvention, and a glimpse of what might rise if we let the compost do its work.

I was still scared. Still grieving. Still unraveling. But I was also planting. And in time, I would see the growth.

BRAND SPOTLIGHT: PANDEMIC BRANDS

The COVID-19 pandemic reshaped branding in real-time. It wasn't logos or slogans that mattered—it was trust, humanity, and presence.

- **Sight**: Empty shelves, taped "X" markers on grocery floors, faces behind masks, logos on Zoom backgrounds instead of event banners. Broadway showcased free performances of shows on live streaming. Live streaming took over the usual movie theatres and purchases of movies. More was available immediately; however, no new productions were being filmed.

- **Sound**: The ding of a Zoom waiting room, claps for healthcare workers at 7 PM, silence of arenas and theaters once roaring with life, professional performers creating music on Zooms like they were singing together

- **Smell:** Bleach, sanitizer, and the smell of baking all day, every day in our kitchen.

- **Touch**: Rubber gloves, elastic mask straps, thermometers constantly against our foreheads, vaccine shots with unknown side effects.

- **Taste:** Takeout in individually wrapped boxes and containers for each item; coffee reheated three times during virtual meetings; yummy desserts made by my daughter and me for neighbors.

The brands that survived—and even thrived—weren't the flashiest. They were the most human. They showed up in the storm, pivoted to meet people's needs, and became part of the survival story.

🔺 Coaching Tips:

1. **Compost the Chaos:** Don't discard your hardest seasons. They can be the richest soil for growth if you let them transform you.

2. **Prioritize Humanity**: In crisis, people don't want perfection. They want progress. They want presence. Your authenticity is your brand.

3. **See the Silver Linings**: Even in global breakdowns, innovation rises. Pay attention to what's being born in the cracks.

4. **Create, Don't Freeze:** Fear paralyzes. Creativity liberates. What small project could you start today that might grow into something big?

Reflection Questions:

1. **What part of your life right now feels like "compost"—messy, decaying, overwhelming?** How might it actually be preparing the soil for something new?

2. **How did the pandemic reshape your view of safety, trust, and community?**

3. **Where can you be more human in your brand or business, showing up imperfect but present?**

Notes:

CHAPTER 10

THE PIVOT SEASON

WHEN CREATIVITY BECAME SURVIVAL

The world was still reeling. Masks dangled from rearview mirrors, hand sanitizer pumps sat like centerpieces on every table, and neighbors waved at each other from six feet apart instead of hugging. My events calendar, once filled with galas and weddings, had been replaced by blank squares and unanswered emails. The silence was suffocating.

But inside our small Scottsdale apartment, something else was stirring.

WHISK IT WITH FLAVA

It began in the kitchen. Flour dusted the counters like snow, butter hissed in pans, and my daughter Ava stood on a stool, her tiny hands gripping a wooden spoon bigger than her arm. "Mom, can we film this one?" she asked, her eyes wide with the confidence only a child could carry. My ten-year-old daughter wanted to be back on camera, teaching others to bake for her YouTube Channel.

And so we did. Our kitchen became a studio. We filmed tutorials, baked themed cakes, and boxed them up for delivery. The sweet smell of vanilla and chocolate drifted through the house, a balm to the anxiety clawing at my chest. When the world outside felt bitter, we delivered sweetness—one cupcake box at a time.

Ava trained privately with a professional French pastry chef, where she learned the true art of baking as a French baker, and wow, was that an experience. Chef Pascal allowed Ava to be the only student during what is normally a twelve-week group weekly course, to twelve days back-to-back with weekends off. It was an insane amount of baking and eating. We videotaped every training, and he gave Ava all his recipes. She alternated with teachers and blew their minds every time, from chocolate eclairs and cream puffs to Paris-Brest cake and fruit tortes to chocolate-and-orange soufflés. When group classes opened, Ava continued learning knife skills, cooking, and baking with other kids.

Neighbors and our leasing office at the apartment complex lit up when Ava showed up with her pastries and cakes. Kids sent messages asking when the next tutorial would be. People were placing orders for their special occasions. Ava and I baked and decorated themed cakes of all kinds, from baby's first to 60th birthdays, from anniversaries to graduations, from get well to first responders. For a moment, we weren't stuck in a pandemic. We were creators. We were givers. We were living, not just surviving. We even had a television show with a green screen where Ava would interview some of my bakers from when I owned Celebrations By Samara in Houston.

THE KAM PROJECT

But we weren't done. She wanted something bigger.

"Mom, can I have a podcast?" I sat on it for a while. It was a lot of work. I was a guest and co-host on events industry podcasts with my long-time friends and photographers (of my wedding and New York City events), Jack Hartzman and Monica Vidal. They introduced me to podcasting since they started one during the pandemic. They became pros and are techy, so they taught me everything about podcasting. During the pandemic, I met Rob Actis in a room on the Clubhouse™ app, and over time, he became one of my dear friends. Rob helped me understand the world of podcasting when I was still learning how to do everything. He is the author of "The Law of Action" and the voice of the "Miracle Morning" audiobooks. Rob sees things others miss, which is why I proclaimed him "the Podcast Whisperer."

THE BIRTH OF A NON-PROFIT

After volunteering at the vaccination site at the stadium on Cameron's birthday, I wanted to do something in honor of my son. Cameron—my son who never got to grow up—was always part of our family's story. Ava wanted to honor him in a way that empowered others. So together, we birthed *The KAM Project*. KAM stands for *Kid Action Makers*™, but Ava suggested changing the "C" to a "K." "It looks cooler and we want kids, not children," she grinned, sketching logo ideas in a notebook on her bed while I lay recovering from a night of volunteering at the State Farm Stadium vaccination site in the pouring rain and February's freezing cold.

The KAM Project became a nonprofit dedicated to helping kids and teens take action. Even during lockdown, we found ways to connect kids who wanted to make a difference—through volunteering, through creativity, through leadership. Watching Ava brainstorm reminded me that resilience isn't just inherited. It's modeled.

KAMcast + KAMcastKIDS

From there, my office transformed —this time into a studio with microphones and headphones. Ava interviewed other kidpreneurs for *KAMcastKIDS*™, her giggles and curiosity leading conversations that inspired peers her age. I hosted *KAMcast*™, where I spoke with entrepreneurs and changemakers who had overcome hardship and built something meaningful.

The hum of the mic, the buzz of the ring light, the sight of my daughter leaning in with confidence on Zoom with a stranger— it was fuel for both of us. We weren't just mother and daughter navigating a pandemic. We were co-creators. Partners in resilience. And it was stressful at times, but also a lot of fun, and we both met incredible people around the globe. Ava even learned to pitch and do introductions in front of adults, Grant Cardone's daughters, and other kidpreneurs.

ACTIONISTALIVE

By spring, the ideas kept multiplying. I launched *ActionistaLIVE LLC.*—my "bucket list actionista" business for dreamers, travelers, and those who wanted to experience more. It wasn't perfect, and it wasn't yet profitable, but it was a possibility. It was a spark of life in a season where so much had died.

Even as the world mourned—people dying alone in hospitals, businesses shuttering, supply chains snapping—I felt the compost doing its work. The decay of what I lost was feeding the soil of what could grow.

And slowly, I began to see: this wasn't just survival. It was a pivot—a season where creativity became the bridge from grief to growth.

BRAND SPOTLIGHT: PODCASTS—VOICES THAT BECAME POWER

Podcasts didn't just grow during the pandemic—they exploded. Suddenly, everyone from celebrities to high school students to global entrepreneurs had a microphone and a message. The world tuned in not just for entertainment, but for connection, education, and authenticity.

- **Sight:** Spare bedrooms turning into podcast studios, waveforms (a graphical representation of a signal that illustrates its variation over time) bouncing across computer screens, and short video clips flooding TikTok™ and Instagram™.

- **Sound:** Raw conversations, unfiltered laughter, whispered late-night recordings, and the kind of storytelling that feels like a friend sitting on your couch, yelling, "quiet on the set in the home."

- **Smell**: Fresh coffee fueling midnight edits, the plastic scent of a new microphone just pulled from the box, home kitchens doubling as recording hubs.

- **Touch:** Fingers tapping "record," headphones snug, mic foam squishy, and the nervous energy of sharing your voice with the world.

- **Taste:** The bittersweet courage of hitting "publish," the thrill of going live, the taste of takeout dinners eaten between editing sessions.

WHY PODCASTS BECAME GAME-CHANGERS

1. **Intimacy + Reach**
   Unlike news soundbites or social media posts, podcasts allow long-form, human conversations. People stuck at home during lockdown craved depth, not just headlines, and podcasts gave them that voice-to-ear intimacy.

2. **The Rise of Influencers as Media**
   Creators like Joe Rogan and Mr. Beast became more than entertainers—they became global media platforms in their own right. During a time when traditional media felt overwhelming or untrustworthy to many, people turned to influencers and podcast hosts for information, community, and inspiration. Mel Robbins became a voice of reason in motherhood.

3. **Clips + Algorithms**
   The podcast wasn't just audio. Episodes turned into bite-sized viral clips shared across TikTok™, YouTube™, and Instagram™. Algorithms loved them —and suddenly, a single moment from a podcast could reach millions in hours.

4. **The New Press Tour**
   For authors, actors, athletes, and entrepreneurs,

podcasts became *the* place to launch ideas, share stories, and connect with new audiences. Being interviewed on the right show often mattered more than traditional press because the audience was more engaged, loyal, and ready to take action.

5. **Everyday Experts Became Brands**
Parents, teachers, bakers, coaches, and even kids with iPads turned their voices into shows. Entire businesses —including ours with *KAMcast* and *KAMcastKIDS*— sprouted from the simple act of sharing stories into a microphone.

MY PIVOT THROUGH PODCASTING

For me, podcasting was oxygen. Ava and I turned our grief into purpose with *The KAM Project* podcasts, building a community from our living room. Guests became collaborators. Listeners became friends. And our voices traveled further than our feet could during a lockdown.

Podcasts weren't just entertainment—they were connection. They were proof that no matter how isolated the world felt, someone out there was listening.

🏆 Coaching Tips:

1. **Treat Creativity as Survival, Not Luxury.**
   When life flips your plans, create anyway. Your next breakthrough might be baked in your kitchen, recorded in your living room, or dreamed up in your journal at midnight. Creativity isn't a hobby—it's oxygen for the soul during chaos.

2. **Let Curiosity Lead the Way.**
   Every pivot begins with a question. "What if we...?" "Could we try...?" "Why not now?" Curiosity is your compass in seasons of uncertainty. Follow what lights you up, even if it doesn't make sense on paper yet.

3. **Build, Don't Wait.**
   You don't need a perfect plan to start. You need motion. The KAM Project, Whisk It With flAVA, and ActionistaLIVE weren't born from certainty—they were born from faith, resourcefulness, and action. Build the bridge as you walk across it.

4. **Let the Next Generation Inspire You.**
   Children don't overthink—they *do*. They remind us of what pure belief looks like. Let their courage reignite yours. Co-create, collaborate, and make space for young voices to lead. Fresh perspectives fuel innovation.

5. **Find Your Frequency.**
   Just like podcasting, your voice has a vibration that attracts your people. When you speak from truth, not perfection, your brand becomes magnetic. Show up in your real voice—shaky, strong, or somewhere in between. That's where connection lives.

6. **Turn Loss Into Launch Fuel.**
   Pain can either pause you or propel you. Let what broke you become the reason you build again. Like compost feeds the soil, your hardships can nourish your next evolution if you let them.

Reflection Questions:

1. **What challenge in your life right now could become your next opportunity?**
   Think of something that feels like an ending. How might it actually be the seed of a new beginning?

2. **How can you turn your home—or current situation —into a creative hub?**
   Wherever you are, innovation can thrive. Your environment doesn't need to be perfect; it just needs intention.

3. **Whose voice are you not hearing enough of— including your own?**
   Are there people in your circle who need space to be

heard—or are you silencing your own ideas before they take shape?

4. **What can you teach, share, or record that could help someone else survive their storm?** Every skill or story you hold can serve as someone else's survival guide. Don't wait to perfect it—press record.

5. **When was the last time you felt fully alive in creation?**
Identify that moment. Now, recreate that feeling—on purpose, this week.

"I no longer wait for perfect timing. I pivot with purpose. I create in the chaos. My ideas are the bridge from who I was to who I am becoming."
Samara Beth

Notes:

A LIFE LIVED EVERYWHERE: HOW I BECAME A REINVENTION MAVERICK

Thirteen cities. Thirty homes. Dozens of lives lived, each one shaped by different walls, zip codes, playgrounds, patios, schools, and friendships that flared up like fireworks, brilliant but sometimes fleeting. Thank goodness for MapQuest™, Google Maps™, and Garmin™ GPS over the years. With my poor sense of direction, learning a new city every year—or every few years—was a crash course in resilience and adaptation. I've made countless wrong turns, packed and unpacked an absurd number of boxes, rebuilt businesses, renovated homes, and rebooted my life more times than most people could imagine.

Let's just say I was one of the hardest friends to keep on a holiday card list. No one could keep up with my moves, and I cycled through emails, phone numbers, and license plates the way hotels cycle through guests. My life was not one straight line but a quilt—stitched together with willpower, innovation, and networking, with a healthy dose of refusing to settle.

Every move carried a price. My kids said goodbye to their best friends again and again, switching schools mid-year, standing in new cafeterias with unfamiliar faces staring back at them. I scrambled to find new doctors, dentists, hairdressers, nail salons, grocery stores, banks, and favorite restaurants. We sold couches and dining sets only to re-buy them later, sometimes from the exact same chain stores. After heirlooms shattered one move too many, we detached ourselves from things and turned to IKEA™, Craigslist™, garage sales, and donations. I became a master at stretching a dollar and, more importantly, at refusing to cry over broken dishes. I did, however, always cry over broken The Pampered Chef™ seasoned stoneware and heirlooms. We lost a lot of both.

Meanwhile, my husband's career—first as a U.S. Navy submarine officer, then in oil and gas—kept him traveling the globe. He was unreachable for months at a time under the ocean, while I held down the fort with pregnancies, kids, jobs, moves, and dreams bigger than midnight. I wore every hat imaginable:

Event Producer. Destination Manager. Meeting Planner. Hair Salon Manager. Resort Clothing Sales Representative. The

Pampered Chef™ Consultant. Fundraiser. Gala Coordinator. Balloon Artist. Barista. Volunteer. Mystery Shopper. Speaker. Fashion Show Developer. Classroom Mom Board Member. Trade Show Exhibitor. Luxury Clothing Store Manager. Director of Events and Catering. CEO. Co-Founder. Carnival Chair. Mom. Wife. Daughter. Nurse. Housekeeper. Cook. Baker.

Whatever the role required, I became it, I freaking owned it like a firecracker.. Rinse. Repeat.

But beneath all those hats, I discovered the golden thread running through every move and every reinvention: Community is not given—it's built.

I didn't wait for people to find me. I found them. I waved first. I knocked on doors with gifts. I held open doors. I hosted block parties before I even knew my neighbors' names. I introduced myself to firefighters, police officers, homeowner associations, teachers, principals, and parents in the carpool lane. People would say, "Samara doesn't know a stranger." That phrase became more than a compliment—it became my lifestyle, my strategy, and eventually, my brand pillar.

I lived by the W.I.N. Principle, especially the "N" for Networking. Not the stiff, transactional version people dread, but networking with warmth, authenticity, and soul. I didn't show up asking what others could do for me. I showed up to give, connect, and serve. And because of that, opportunities opened. Doors I didn't even know existed swung wide. Stages invited me. Magazines featured me. Clients came. Referrals multiplied.

Every city, every move, every challenge demanded reinvention. I didn't just become resilient—I became a "Reinvention Maverick." Not because I wanted to, but because life gave me no choice. Over time, I realized home isn't four walls. Home is the people you gather, the light you carry, and the circles you choose to build.

I often think of that phrase: "Home is where the heart is." For me, it's not so simple. I've lived everywhere. My home is in the friendships that last across decades and zip codes. The kind of friends you can go years without speaking to, then pick up right where you left off. The kind you run into later in life, and though everything has changed, they still see *you* without judgment. That's home.

And here's the truth I learned: you are your brand everywhere you go. Your introduction, your handshake, your laughter, your resilience—it all precedes you. So be intentional. Carry a brand you're proud of.

BRAND SPOTLIGHT: LEGO®

LEGO® isn't just a toy. It's a **global brand of reinvention.**

In our house, LEGO® was more than entertainment—it was identity. My son memorized every set like scripture. Piece counts, prices, release schedules, and catalog errors (which he would correct in crayon and send to LEGO® corporate). He'd spend hours in the LEGO® store, pointing out sets to employees, proudly reciting details like a tiny walking catalog. Now, at twenty-one, he still only wants LEGO®.

My daughter, Ava, joined in by building LEGO® at a young age as well. Determined to be like her big brother, they built the LEGO® Disney Castle inspired by *Cinderella Castle* together and blew us away. Now she builds LEGO botanicals for me—roses, orchids, bonsai trees. Because she knows her mama can't keep real plants alive, she gifted me gardens I couldn't kill. And once, she built me a LEGO® bamboo structure, which now sits in my office. My daily reminder: even resilience can be built brick by brick.

That's the brilliance of LEGO®. It doesn't just entertain—it teaches patience, perseverance, creativity, and reinvention. You break things apart, you start over, you rebuild. And in that rebuilding, you create something new, often stronger, sometimes more imaginative than before.

For me, LEGO® mirrors the Reinvention Maverick journey. Life knocked me down, scattered my pieces across the floor.

But each move, each loss, each new start gave me a chance to rebuild. You may use the step-by-step instructions that come with the box (what we call a framework or playbook), or you may use your imagination to craft your own creation, not into the same thing you had before, but into something different, creative, resilient, and beautiful.

Just like LEGO®.

- **Sight**: Colorful bricks scattered across the carpet, half-built castles, superhero ships, and dream cities waiting to be finished.

- **Sound**: The satisfying *snap* of two bricks locking together, the clatter of pieces tumbling from a plastic bin, the crash when a tower topples.

- **Touch**: The rough edge of a single brick pressed into your palm, the smooth connection of a new wall forming.

- **Smell**: Fresh plastic and cardboard from a newly opened box.

- **Taste**: The sweetness of imagination—dreams coming to life piece by piece.

🚢 **Coaching Tips:**

1. **Arrive with Energy**: In every new city or room, enter with warmth and authenticity. Your energy introduces your brand before your words do.

2. **Reframe Transitions as Opportunities**: Every pivot isn't an ending—it's a chance to redesign your life, brick by brick.

3. **Network Through Service**: Lead with generosity. Ask, "How can I support you?" before you ask, "What's in it for me?"

4. **Embody Resilience Publicly**: When you model grace under pressure, you don't just survive—you teach others how to thrive.

5. **Build Like LEGO®**: Don't fear breaking down. It's part of the design. Each rebuild can be better, stronger, and more aligned.

Reflection Questions:

1. **What parts of your identity have stayed with you through every reinvention?**

2. **Where in your life can you start seeing "chaos" as the scattered pieces of a new design?**

3. **Who do you need to surround yourself with to help you build your next great structure—your legacy?**

Notes:

SECTION 4

EMPOWERED TO EMPOWER

UNLOCK YOUR OWN BADASS BAMBOO

CREATE YOUR BAMBOO BLUEPRINT™

. . . .

This chapter is your invitation to pause, reflect, and build your own Bamboo Blueprint™, which is your guide (or roadmap) to growing, bending, and thriving through every storm.

I want to take you back to a moment…

My Mom called us and said, "Daddy is having a stroke, come now!" We rushed to their house. The paramedics had him in a gurney by the time we arrived, and he was unable to speak. Despite my mom begging the paramedics to take him to the hospital five minutes further to the stroke ward, the ambulance insisted on taking my dad to their preferred hospital. My daughter, boyfriend, and I rushed to the hospital shortly after his CAT scan, only for him to be taken to the hospital that my mom had initially insisted they take him to.

It was so hot in Arizona that day; we were living on candy, water, protein bars, and no sleep. I was able to gather some people to help us move to the area, including neighbors and my brother, who flew in from California for Dad.

I was standing in my third bedroom, which also served as my home office, in the thirteenth city of my thirtieth home, staring at more stacks of boxes reaching the ceiling, packing paper piled higher than my five-foot frame, dirty floors, and a general mess. My daughter was asleep in another new room—again. That was the moment I had to decide: break or bend. [Enter waterworks]. The exhaustion, sadness, and fear took over my body, and I had a complete mental breakdown. The stress, fear, and worry of me starting a new business again if things did not work out at my current job (Director of Events & Catering at a venue), which provided my income.

Like when I started Celebrations By Samara in 2009, while juggling grief from losing Cameron, a high-risk, scary pregnancy with Ava, new schools for Gavin, and countless moves. That business was born from my need to create joy even while navigating loss. Over the years, I rebuilt repeatedly, producing award-winning events, flying between states and provinces, sleeping on airbeds or my friends' kids' beds, and building new communities. This chapter is about helping you choose to bend, grow, and rise, just as I did.

THE BAMBOO BLUEPRINT™: RESILIENCE IN MOTION

If the W.I.N. Framework is the engine, then the **Bamboo Blueprint™** is the architecture—the structural design of resilience itself. Bamboo doesn't grow overnight. It spends its first years developing roots so deep that when it finally shoots upward, it grows fast, strong, and nearly unbreakable.

Bamboo Blueprint Success = Resilience + Backbone + Strength + Conviction.

Let's break that down:

Resilience—The ability to bend without breaking. When the winds of life whip through your plans, resilience is what keeps you upright. It's not resistance; it's response. Bamboo doesn't fight the storm. It sways with it—absorbing, adapting, and returning stronger when the skies clear.

Backbone—The inner structure that holds you steady when emotions try to pull you apart. In business and life, your backbone is your standards—your non-negotiables. It's the reason you say "no" to what doesn't align, even when "yes" might look easier in the moment—recovering "people pleaser" over here. Sound like someone you know?

Strength—True strength isn't about how heavy you can lift; it's about what you can carry without complaint. It's knowing when to push through, when to pause, and when to delegate.

Strength is the quiet discipline of staying consistent—even when no one's clapping.

Conviction—This is the fire inside the fiber—the "why" that fuels the work. Conviction is your emotional spine—the belief that your purpose matters even when no one else sees it yet. When you have conviction, you believe that your abilities can help and serve others. Confidence comes with conviction. When resilience, backbone, and strength fuse with conviction, you stop surviving and start thriving.

That's your Bamboo Blueprint. It's not just a mindset—it's a model for growth. It's how you turn chaos into compost, fear into focus, and storms into stories that inspire.

When you begin to view your life through this lens, you'll realize that every challenge, every pivot, and every moment of exhaustion was laying the groundwork for your next expansion. Just like the bamboo's roots, your foundation grows underground—unseen, but unstoppable.

Community and positive, calming energy are crucial for getting through hard times. Like he always does, my boyfriend recognized my fear of losing my dad, my stress over moving apartments in extreme heat, and two fewer helpers (mom and dad), so he pulled me into an embrace to keep me focused and my mind calm, and then he went to run errands. I went into my master bedroom to organize my closet. I started to get increasingly tired and drained, which was understandable from my past days. I ultimately passed out; my daughter fell asleep with her legs dangling off her bed, and I laid down to nap in my closet.

What I didn't realize until the next day was that the new washing machine and dryer installed by the apartment complex had been leaking gas for two days. My neighbor helped us move my balcony furniture and immediately smelled the gas. Not one apartment maintenance staff member came to my home to answer my calls. However, the gas company rushed over as soon as possible. The dryer was improperly installed with a broken tube, and a thousand cubic feet of gas were measured in my three-bedroom apartment, with even more in surrounding areas and apartments. The gas company could smell it from the parking lot. We were so immune to it from the days of moving and the door opening and closing that by the time the apartment complex emergency maintenance showed up, we would have blown up the block if we had lit a candle or turned on the gas stove.

We kept doors and windows open and kept unpacking and visiting my parents in the hospital. There was no stopping. There was no breathing time. It was go-go-go. And certainly not the first time, or fifth time, or even 100th time that I have been in a go-go-go scenario.

I could have crumbled. But I remembered: I bend, but I don't break. Like bamboo. That's why bamboo plants are throughout my home. They are a reminder to me that "I got this."

This chapter is about helping you choose to bend, grow, and rise, just as I did. So, I keep my life saver nearby. So, here is a reminder of the W.I.N. Framework and ways to brainstorm and execute it in your story. When you recognize and tell your story, people find you authentic, gain a visual of where you came from, and understand how you got to where you are.

Your signature talk encompasses your personal story and business journey—the pain points and the misconceptions, and what you learned from the ebbs and flows, the failures and successes. Then, you take the successes and create teaching moments from them to help remind yourself and teach others to do the same.

THE W.I.N. FRAMEWORK

Willpower: Identify where you've shown up, even when it was hard.

I recall moments where I refused to give up. For example, when I launched Celebrations By Samara in a challenging market after the 2008 market crash and Hurricane Ike destroyed our city, or when I navigated a tough client situation, I demonstrated resilience and adaptability.

- **List three moments where you persevered and what you learned.**

Innovation: Identify creative avenues you can take when what you are doing is simply not working.

I recall the pivots I made, such as embracing virtual events during the pandemic and helping others realize their dreams, just as I did with Ava's bakery dreams during the 2020 COVID pandemic.

- **Write down three instances in which you approached challenges differently, created something new, or adapted your path.**

Networking: Identify your networks (big and small, local and national, global and digital).

The silver lining of the pandemic is that the entire world went through it together. The world shut down. Digital social audio apps (like the Clubhouse app), video channels (like YouTube), course creation, and AI (artificial intelligence) emerged like never before. Use them to help you network and work faster. But, be sure to work smarter and keep the real-life networking going as you build, grow, and create your 10X Super Life (Grant Cardone).

When I consider my networks, I think of the people I met along the way: friends, clients, colleagues, co-chairs, neighbors, school groups who became my extended family, and clients and referrers. The people in my event industry were like my family away from home. I would join local industry meetings and events, as well as organizations, and become as active as possible in various networking groups and non-profit organizations to make new friends, connections, and clients.

- **Name three relationships that helped you grow. Note what you learned and how you can be more intentional in building your circles.**

MAP YOUR STORY

Chart your journey: Where you began, the storms you survived, the milestones you reached, and the ways you bent but did not break. Notice how each chapter in your story has built your strength and resilience. When you amplify your brand through your story as a speaker, that's where the magic begins.

BUILD YOUR BRAND

Once you've crafted your story, it's time to share it and build your brand. Start by incorporating your story into your social media bios, website, media kit, pitch decks, and elevator pitches. Have a 30-second, 60-second, 90-second, and signature ready to go. Use a teleprompter app if you need it in front of you.

Create video clips sharing parts of your journey. Use client testimonials that align with your values. Provide tips for collecting video testimonials and endorsements so it's quick and straightforward for people who know and have worked with you to endorse you. Host small gatherings or virtual events where you speak about your experience and invite others to connect. Partner with local businesses or charities to grow your network.

Most importantly, show up consistently and authentically.

Listen, you don't need to be a motivational speaker to motivate, or a sports coach to give a pep talk. Every day, as a parent, employer, colleague, or friend, you can use these same skills to uplift, encourage, and inspire. Whether it's helping a child believe in themselves, supporting a co-worker through challenges, empathizing with a friend who is pregnant with a sick baby, or reassuring a client, your words and energy have the power to change lives.

You've got this. Step into your Badass Bamboo. Let's W.I.N. together. You are never "alone." I'm only an email, a call, or a live event away.

BONUS – TESTIMONIAL ASK SCRIPT

This is a "Testimonial Ask" that I keep readily available in the "notes" of my phone. You can fill in the blanks and copy and paste to people you know, or you can add to a pop-up when a client pays. Regardless, feel free to take from this what you think would best represent your brand. We have a frame in Canva that we drop the videos into.

Hi _____,

Since we have a working relationship, I am asking if you would help me with marketing my global audience for my business, _____. Would you please submit a video testimonial for my branding team to use on my marketing materials and videos?

*We would like to ask if you could **record a short video** (on your phone or using Zoom on your computer is perfect), sharing your biggest "aha!" moment.*

Here is a little guideline in case you need some help:

- Introduction with your company name.
- Where you are from.
- I participated in the _____ in person or virtually or I know me from _____
- My main aha moment/lesson I walked away with was...
- From that I have created x result.
-You can speak on my energy, character, commitment, capability, work ethic, results, memories, and/or best thing about working with me.
- I recommend you participate in _____ programs, hire _____ to speak, coach or craft and produce your events.

Thank you for being such a great addition to our community. We look forward to seeing you at our upcoming events.

A couple of tips:

-It's important that you try to use natural or good lighting, but don't stress over it.
-Please film horizontally just like I am in this How-To video.

-Clear and Concise is perfect. No more than 45 seconds is great!

As a special thank you for taking time out to participate, I will email you a free _____

Don't forget to subscribe at _____ so I have an email to send it to.

Follow, Like, and Comment @_____ on social media, and we will tag you when we post your testimonial video.

🎄 Coaching Tips:

Let me help you define your *Flexibility, Grit, and Growth Strategy*:

1.   Where can you let go of rigidity and become more flexible? Being fluid is crucial in many industries and positions.

2.   What areas require more grit, hustle, and determination?

3.   How will you nurture your growth over the next year? Reverse engineer your next twelve months by starting with visualizing where you want to see yourself in twelve months. Then, work backwards, dividing out the months, weeks, days, and hours to determine what you realistically need to do, hour by hour, each day, to accomplish that goal.

4.   Write down three ways you will share your story this month, then schedule them on your calendar and commit to them.

Reflection Questions:

1. Journal about a recent challenge and how you responded.

2. Write a letter to yourself, acknowledging your resilience. Seal it, address the envelope, put a stamp on it, and kindly instruct someone who is completely dependable to mail it in six months.

3. List three commitments to your growth, flexibility, and community-building.

4. List twenty individuals you can contact today to request a testimonial from. Clients, vendors, friends, collaborators. No one can discount your mom ;-)

Notes:

CHAPTER 13

YOU ARE A BADASS BAMBOO

There are two kinds of final chapters: The kind that drifts to black like end credits, and the kind that feels like a door kicked open to morning air. I want this one to be the second kind—the chapter you can smell, touch, hear, and step into.

Close your eyes for a breath. Hear the hush right before a curtain rises. Smell fresh coffee on a clean, ordinary Monday. Feel the cool weight of a pen in your hand. That hum in your chest is not nerves. It is potential, gathering itself.

This is the moment where some people file for Chapters 3, 11, or 13 (depending on the individual or the business)—the legal kind that signals collapse. I am here to invite you to write a very different chapter—the personal kind that announces conviction. Instead of declaring bankruptcy, you declare backbone. Instead of liquidation, you choose liberation. This chapter is not a ledger of losses. It is a balance sheet of lessons, paid for with sweat, tears, and the kind of love that keeps showing up after the party is over. Note that I am not a financial advisor, planner, or CPA. This is not legal or financial advice; it is strictly for motivational purposes.

Remember that you are the embodiment of Badass Bamboo. You have bent, but you have not broken. You have staggered through fluorescent hospital lights and kept moving. You have packed boxes by moonlight, folded courage into carry-ons, and rearranged your life around kids, clients, and crises completely out of your control. You have cooked hope in borrowed kitchens, prayed in parked cars, and answered emails with swollen eyes and sweaty palms. You have built communities with house parties and introductions with pure joy. You have learned to make a room warmer by walking into it with your light and positive energy. You have shown up when others would quit, adapted when others froze, and you've built communities, brands, and dreams even through grief, fear, and exhaustion.

Be honest with yourself for one heartbeat longer. You did not "bounce back." You bounced forward. You turned storms into compost. You turned silence into strategy. You turned broke into bending. You turned pain into a platform and a plan.

Note: I wrote Chapter 13 up to this point while tears were pouring out of my eyes. I'm not perfect. There are times when I need to hear this myself. I wrote this book for myself as much as for you. We all need reminders.

If you have read to this point, you already belong to a rare tribe. The tribe that finishes. The tribe that does the last rep when no one is watching. The tribe that measures progress in quiet promises kept to itself. You are proof that attention can still be sustained, that discipline can still be trained, and that long-form focus can still shape a long-game life.

So, before you close this book, let's engrave your **Bamboo Blueprint™** into muscle memory:

- **Resilience**: You bend with the wind; you do not beg it to stop.

- **Backbone**: You keep your standards when the room gets loud.

- **Strength**: You carry what matters and set down what does not.

- **Conviction**: You move like someone who knows why and how.

That is what keeps you from filing for the wrong "chapter." That is what turns your Chapter 13 into a manifesto, not a surrender.

YOUR SENSES ARE YOUR COMPASS

When life starts to tilt, return to the senses. They are anchors and alarms.

- **Sight**: Post your promise where you can see it—one sentence on a sticky note by the sink. When the water runs in the morning, you read it out loud. That is how momentum begins.

- **Sound**: Build a soundtrack that summons your future. Put three songs on repeat that make you move your shoulders and lift your chin. Movement is medicine.

- **Touch**: Hold your tools. The pen that signs your new offer. The microphone that shares your story. The keyboard that publishes your pitch. Touch creates trust with yourself.

- **Smell**: Light a candle that smells like fresh start—citrus, rain, cedar. It will become the scent memory of your new chapter.

- **Taste**: Celebrate small wins with something simple and intentional. A square of dark chocolate after the outreach is done. A toast with sparkling flavored water or champagne when the proposal is sent. Train your brain to love follow-through.

YOUR W.I.N. STILL WINS

You already know the framework: **Willpower, Innovation, Networking**. Let's lock it in for your next twelve months.

- **Willpower**: Commit to showing up at the same time every day for the next ninety days. Even fifteen focused minutes will change your life if you stack them. Put it on the calendar and protect it with teeth.

- **Innovation**: Create one experiment every month. A new offer, a new room, a new stage, a new partnership, a new format. Innovation is curiosity with a deadline.

- **Networking**: Choose your five. Five humans you will champion, learn from, and collaborate with. Send one meaningful message a day, five days a week. In one year, you will have made 250 quality touches. Doors open for the consistent and the generous.

THE PROMISE YOU WRITE TODAY

On a plain sheet of paper, write this sentence in your own hand:

"I do not file for Chapter 11. I write Chapter 11. I am Badass Bamboo—resilient in the wind, rooted in the storm, rising in the sun."

Read it twice. Fold it once. Put it where your hand will find it tomorrow.

WHAT YOU LEAVE IN THE ROOM

Legacy is not a bronze plaque. Legacy is residue. It is the warmth people feel when you have left the room. It is the clarity you lend to those who are still fogged by fear. It is the courage your kids borrow because they saw you tell the truth, keep the promise, and apologize when you are late picking them up, or mess up. It is the vendor you paid on time, the client you coached with care, the stranger you welcomed as if they mattered—because they do matter.

When you walk into a meeting, bring quiet confidence and clean energy.

When you pitch, tell the story that costs you something and gives the listener everything.

When you build, choose the sustainable solution even if it is slower. When you scale, take people with you. Badass is not noise. Badass is stewardship. Productivity is sexy!

IF TODAY IS HEAVY

If your chest is tight right now, place a palm there. Feel the drum that has carried you through every chapter. Inhale for four, hold for four, exhale for six. Again. Again. The room will widen. The next step will appear. Your future does not need you to be fearless. It needs you to be faithful—one small brave thing, repeated.

YOUR CLOSING CEREMONY

Stand up. Literally stand. Shoulders back. Feet grounded. Say your full name out loud.

Then say: "I am writing my chapters! I am writing my story! I bend. I rise. I build. I belong. I am Badass Bamboo."

Let the words settle. Let them echo. Let them become how you answer the door when opportunity knocks.

THREE ACTIONS BEFORE SUNSET

Write these by hand, then do them before the day ends:

1. **Reach Out**: Send one message to someone who can open a door and one message to someone for whom you can open a door. Generosity creates gravity.

2. **Ship One Thing**: Publish the post, send the pitch, book the room, order the microphone, register the domain, schedule the call. Done is a dopamine signal.

3. **Plant One Root**: Block tomorrow's power hour on your calendar. Name it. Guard it. Treat it like revenue, because it will be.

THIS IS NOT THE END; THIS IS NOT GOODBYE

To get inspired, unplug and read educational professional development books while others read romance and mystery. Listen to uplifting podcasts instead of true crime and biased news.

Be the one percenter who finishes, who grows, who scales, who succeeds, and most importantly, who gives back. "Give, give, give," as Grant Cardone says. I became a 10X Certified Business Coach and Licensee with Grant Cardone, so I could learn to go from decades as a consultant to coaching and helping other businesses as a business coach. It adds education and value in sales, marketing, and mindset. Creating a "10X® Super Life" is not a pipe dream; it's a target. What if you were able to join different groups and take the courses that align with you and your business? You would make new friends and connections at the same time, and add so much value to your services and your team.

When you lay this book down, I want you to feel the electric quiet of a stage just before the lights come up. The boardroom before you pitch your presentation. The podcast before you hear, "Quiet on the set!"

The bamboo forests that survive a century do not announce themselves. They simply keep growing. So will you.

Show up. Speak true. Build well. Love wide. Finish what you start. Begin again when you do not. And when the wind rises, smile. You were made for weather.

You are not filing for Chapter 11. You are writing Chapter 11. You are the author, the architect, the rooted one, the rising one. You are the author of your story.

Take a moment to honor your journey. Be above the rest. Show your light energy when you walk into a room and own it. Network, build powerful relationships, and make those five to seventeen touches it requires to make a sale, or have someone fall in love with you and make a lifelong commitment. Every twist, every storm, every triumph. This is your legacy. And now, step forward. Share your story authentically. In order to become your authentic self, you have to go through the trials and tribulations in life. You are on the right track.

You're on the right track.

Show up. Showing up is the first act of courage that turns possibility into reality. Inspire others not by being perfect, but by being present, resilient, and real.

You are the light others need to see.

You are the example others crave.

Be like Bamboo.

You are Badass Bamboo.

Now go WIN your life.

ACTION STEPS

1. Take Action: Email us your three action steps to *brands@samarabethandco.com* so we can cheer you on and hold you to your greatness.

2. Tag *@samarabethandco* in your social media posts sharing how your personal and business brands have flourished during this process.

3. Check out our evergreen and group courses and see which would help you take the next step.

4. Go to our **Amazon Author's page** and see which books and workbooks you can order to help your journey continue to grow in strength and knowledge. (*www.amazon.com/stores/Samara-Beth/author/ B0DK2Q6JKG*)

Notes:

THE W.I.N.N.I.N.G. BRAND FRAMEWORK

From "Invisible to Iconic" —this is the real playbook.

You don't stumble into icon status—you script it. This isn't just a theory. This is the framework that's taken authors from self-doubt to six-figure book launches, speakers from "what stage" to Times Square jumbotrons, and brands from DIY confusion to network news features, sold-out retreats, and inboxes overflowing with opportunity.

This chapter? It's the part most people gatekeep. It's the secret sauce.

I'm giving it to you.

Because if you've made it this far, you're not here to blend in —you're here to become unforgettable.

Your Brand Has DNA. Let's code it.

What you're about to read is the behind-the-scenes framework we use at Samara Beth & Co. to transform brilliant but invisible entrepreneurs into celebrity-level brands—without the burnout, gimmicks, or fake-fame filters.

This is the system that aligns your message, mission, media, and momentum, so your story isn't just seen—it's shared, booked, quoted, and paid.

Ready?

Let's decode your W.I.N.N.I.N.G. moment.

W — Wake the Brand

Before you brand anything, you want to wake up to what you're really here to say. This is where we begin. We strip away the noise, the imposter syndrome, the recycled bios and generic pitches, and we go deeper. Sometimes emotionally deep.

What do you stand for?

What do you refuse to apologize for?

What movement are you quietly building but haven't fully claimed?

In this phase, we shape your mission, movement, and manifesto; your audience psychology and buying behavior; and your positioning that makes you unignorable. This is where your story stops blending and starts cutting through.

I — Identity & Influence

Your brand's look should feel like a visual exhale—like yes, that's me. Now we design the soul of your brand—the visual and verbal DNA that makes you recognizable in a scroll, on a billboard, or from the back of a room. This is more than logos. It's language. It's emotional resonance. It's consistent across everything, from your speaker deck to your social media to your swag bag at a luxury retreat.

This is why we shared the sensory experiences tied to the iconic brands throughout this book. They last lifetimes, because they understand their customer and use sensory marketing, which makes their brands nostalgic in time.

Clients who work with Samara Beth & Co. walk away with:

1. Logo suite, color palette, and brand fonts with intentional psychology
2. Signature tone and content pillars
3. Custom moodboard and aesthetic system
4. Branded visual assets ready for omnipresence

N — Narrative Authority

Facts tell. But stories? Stories make people feel something. That's power. Your story isn't "just" a story. It's the strategy behind your audience trusting you over anyone else.

Here, we craft your:

1. Signature origin story (Overcome → Outcome)
2. Stage and podcast bio and media kit one-pager that gets you booked
3. Reel and trailer video scripts that magnetize your message
4. Hero hooks and brand soundbites you can say in your sleep
5. We don't just write words—we build a storybank you'll pull from for years to come

N — Network Visibility

You don't need more hustle. You need more eyes. The right eyes. This is where we stop posting and praying and start building real visibility ecosystems. We've placed clients on television, radio, podcast networks, and massive digital platforms. We've built brands that go from idea to Times Square billboard in less than six months. And yes—your content will look like a magazine spread, not a Canva square.

In this phase:

1. We design your media kit and speaker assets
2. We secure visibility stacking: press, panels, influencer collabs
3. We script your "I'm ready for press" moment—and train you for it
4. You will no longer be the best-kept secret in your industry

I — Icon Status Activation

The most iconic brands don't hustle harder. They launch with intention. Here's where we activate.

Visualize: You, standing confidently in a brand shoot, not awkwardly adjusting your shirt. You, delivering a stage talk that lands. You, signing a client while your pre-scheduled reel hits 10K views. Your book is on a tablet on the nightstand of your vacation room, provided by a luxury hotel.

In our Authority Launch Plan:

1. We map your signature brand content across channels
2. We align digital + in-person visibility
3. We implement your sales system—without feeling "salesy"
4. We use a laddered approach: Do-It-Yourself → Done-With-You → Done-For-You

So, no matter your bandwidth, your brand builds without burnout.

N — Networked Expansion

Your brand doesn't scale through hustle. It scales through humans. Not to say that we do not hustle, because we most certainly do. But we hustle smarter. We help you curate your power crew: mentors, media allies, and brand collabs that multiply your exposure and impact.

This is where we build your Influence Map and expand your orbit, through:

1. Joint venture strategies and influencer activations
2. High-converting events (live and virtual)
3. Thought-leadership positioning that earns respect—and revenue
4. Connections in our global ecosystem
5. Remember: Networks create net worth

G — Give Legacy

You're not just building a brand. You're building what outlives you. Here's where we turn your voice into volume:

Your book becomes your new business card.

Your retreat becomes your movement.

Your media becomes your magnet.

You'll launch (or level up):

1. Your legacy project—book, docuseries, event, podcast, television show
2. Your evergreen brand ecosystem
3. Your unforgettable presence

And most importantly, your audience will finally know who the hell you are—and why you matter. You can be the next household name when you follow the framework and have a team there for you as you grow and reach business breakpoints.

You're not waiting for "One Day." You're writing your day one. You've already done the hard work. You've built something great. Now, it's time to make it iconic—strategically, beautifully, profitably.

This framework isn't just a flowchart. It's the new standard for building a personal and business brand that sells, scales, and stays remembered. Because when your message is clear, your brand is aligned, and your story is strategic. You don't need to chase influence. You become it.

Your next move is to decide whether you want to do all this on your own or have a team of professionals behind you every step of the way.

Let Samara Beth & Co. map your story, brand, and strategy—so your next move isn't just a post... It's a power play.

Scan this QR code to receive a d**igital download** of our **WINNING Framework** to implement for your personal and/ or business brand.

Notes:

SAMARA BETH

Samara Beth, affectionately known as "Lil' Bamboo" for her resilience and adaptability, is a powerhouse in the world of events, branding, coaching, and transformation. With over thirty years of experience, she has carved out a name for herself as a national award-winning event producer, branding coach, consultant, and developer, a 10X certified business coach and licensee with self-made billionaire Grant Cardone, #1 bestselling author, marketing, public relations, press expert, and keynote speaker.

As the founder of Samara Beth & Co., she combines her passion for events with a mission to inspire resilience and personal transformation, teaching others how to turn life's challenges into powerful personal and business brands.

Samara Beth's career began in the fast-paced field of event planning, where she organized large-scale corporate, social, and nonprofit events across North America. Her journey spans roles from managing major corporate conventions and shareholders' meetings to orchestrating intimate retreats and kids' birthday parties. She has produced meetings, events, and destination management services for Johnson & Johnson, American Express, Coca-Cola, national banks and credit unions, network marketing companies, food and beverage global services, oil and gas industries, real estate agencies, Wall Street firms, and nearly every major pharmaceutical company.

Samara Beth's former brand, Celebrations By Samara, made her known for her meticulous attention to detail, her talent for bringing visions to life, and her knack for creating memorable experiential themes. Samara Beth has earned national accolades, including multiple industry awards for "Best Team Event" and "Best Social Event," as well as recognition as a "Top National Recruiter" for The Pampered Chef, and philanthropic awards such as the "Volunteer Spirit Award" and the "Humanitarian Award."

Yet, Samara Beth's purpose extends far beyond event production. Having lived in thirteen cities and thirty homes, often as a military and expat spouse, she's no stranger to the transformative power of resilience, which has given her the tools to coach others. This deep-rooted adaptability earned her the nickname "Lil' Bamboo" and has become the heart of her coaching philosophy.

Through personal challenges, including navigating her children's severe health issues and constantly moving business and family, Samara Beth learned firsthand the importance of community, purpose, and self-belief. Her commitment to teaching businesses and entrepreneurs to WIN is now a cornerstone of her own business, where she coaches individuals on embracing resilience and transformation as foundations for authentic personal and business brands.

As a business coach and keynote speaker, Samara Beth is dedicated to helping others uncover their potential by transforming personal obstacles into powerful, brand-defining stories and becoming omnipresent. She empowers her clients to build authentic brands that resonate deeply with their audiences.

Her expertise in transformation and branding comes to life in her signature programs: "The Badass Bamboo Blueprint," "Paid to Vacation—Retreat Revenue Masterclass," "Networking with Intention" workshop, "The Brand Experience Blueprint," and the "WIN Method Authority Blueprint." Through these offerings, along with her widely recognized "TRIPS Blueprint" workshops, Samara shares actionable strategies for planning unforgettable events, building resilient brands, and leading with integrity and adaptability.

Samara Beth's motivating energy is contagious, her empathy unmatched, and her message clear: resilience and transformation are not just personal victories; they are the bedrock of a compelling, authority-driven brand. Her 'done for you' branding, events, and social media services, workshops, and retreats provide the tools, community, and confidence needed to cultivate such a brand, guiding her clients on a path where business success and personal fulfillment meet.

Through Samara Beth & Co., Samara Beth continues her mission to help others realize their potential, set ambitious goals, take action, and celebrate each milestone along the way. Her journey is one of perseverance, reinvention, and a relentless commitment to growth. She does this work because she knows, firsthand, that resilience transforms lives, and that every event, retreat, and brand has the potential to inspire lasting change.

This is Samara Beth's calling, and it's what fuels her every day.

Thank you for being a part of our Bamboo Forest.

Stay Connected

Personal Brand:

SamaraBeth.com

- 1:1 and Group Business and Events Coaching
- Branding and Events Courses
- Book Samara Beth for Speaking Opportunities

Business Brand:

SamaraBethandCo.com

WINNING Your Brand with Branding, Media, and Social Domination:

- Done-For-You Branding
- Social Media Services
- Book bestseller promotion and placement services
- Full-Service Events, Retreats, and Summit Production
- Become a bestseller in digital, print, and audiobook formats month after month:
    - Verified Reviews on Amazon and Barnes & Noble
    - Written and Submitted Editorials
    - Written and Submitted Press Articles about you and your book(s)
    - Promotional Marketing Deck to use for your own marketing and sales purposes
    - Strategic Book Placement in luxury hotels beside tablets, AirBnBs, hospitals, recovery centers, cafes, media, libraries, book stores of all sizes, and more…

Follow us:

Instagram: @SamaraBethandCo
Facebook: @SamaraBethandCompany
LinkedIn: @SamaraHurley
YouTube: @SamaraBethandCo.com

Send us an email:

Events Team   *events@samarabethandco.com*
Branding Team   *brands@samarabethandco.com*

Be Like Badass Bamboo!

Team@IntegrityPub.com
www.IntegrityPublishingInternational.com